It's Raining
Cats and Dogs

It's Raining
Cats and Dogs

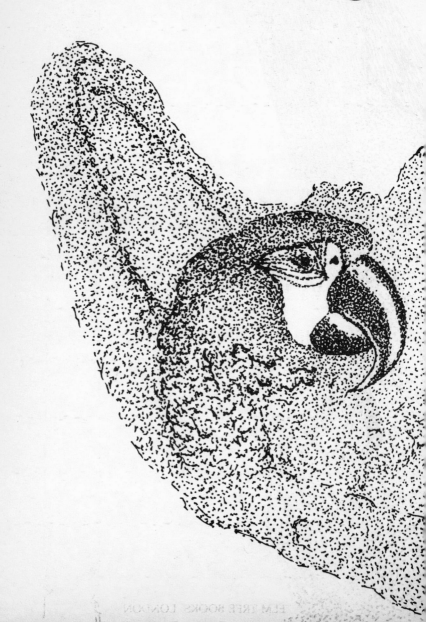

ELM TREE BOOKS LONDON

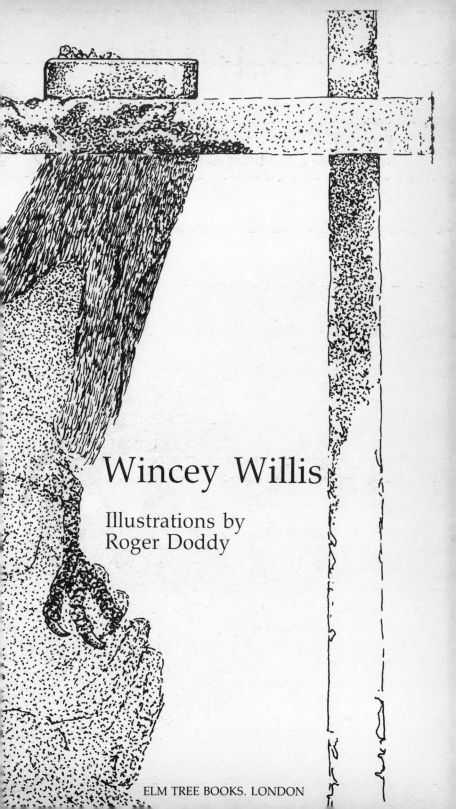

Wincey Willis

Illustrations by
Roger Doddy

ELM TREE BOOKS. LONDON

To my Mother with love
And my Father, who influenced me
more than he will ever know. I miss you.

Thanks to all the brilliant ladies and gentlemen of the veterinary
profession who have helped me over the years.

First published in Great Britain 1986
by Hamish Hamilton Ltd/Elm Tree Books Ltd
27 Wrights Lane London W8 5TZ

British Library Cataloguing in Publication Data

Willis, Wincey
    It's raining cats and dogs.
    1. Animal culture
    I. Title
    636.08'3   SF76.5

    ISBN 0–241–11848–4

Phototypeset by Input Typesetting Ltd, London
Printed and bound in Great Britain by
Billing and Sons Ltd, Worcester

Contents

Foreword

I think most people are animal freaks in one way or another and certainly it is not confined to colour, class or creed. I know of an Amerindian woman in Guyana who thought more of her Red Howler Monkey than of her husband. Having inspected both primates, I was inclined to agree with her. I know of an old lady who, every Saturday evening, got quietly and joyously drunk on home-made parsnip wine with her two cockatoos. I know of a man who carries his favourite snake around in a Gladstone bag and produces it at dinner parties, to the consternation of all non-herpetologists present and yet another, whose passion for snakes was so great that he had to buy the house next door, for his own was so full of serpents there was no room for him. I know of a man who cannot go on holiday with his wife as there would be no-one to look after his hedgehogs and other insectivores. I get regular letters from an old lady living in a high-rise flat in Moscow on the subject of her marmosets, and another lady living in a super luxury apartment in Geneva who has a gigantic iguana instead of a dog or a cat. The desire to have other animals around you seems to be universal and thus, one presumes, were the first dogs and cats, cows and pigs and sheep added to man's family.

This, then, is a book about an animal freak and you have been warned, though I am sure that you will find it as charming as I did and recognise yourself on every other page.

Gerald Durrell.

23rd April 1986

Introduction

For as long as I can remember I have been fascinated by the living creatures around me. I've never suffered the common fear of spiders and actively sought out the company of snakes. When given a doll's tea set as a small child, I only ever used the plates and dishes. These were my feed dishes in my pretend zoo. The cups were discarded as I carried my make-believe food to my cuddly toys held captive in cages made up of old egg-boxes. As I grew older and more responsible I was allowed to start my own collection of the real thing. As long as I promised to take sole charge of whatever pet I had set my heart on, I was given quite a free hand. My father, being a man of the country, taught me a lot and my mother resigned herself to the regular procession of new arrivals. Most were kept in the garden or the cabin which my father had built, but slowly they encroached into Mother's territory indoors. Cleanliness is next to godliness, they say – if it is so, my Mum must have a guaranteed place in heaven. Cleanliness is next to impossible for me, but for my animals nothing is too good. I always kept their cages immaculate, so we rarely fell out over the indoor creatures.

Wherever I have lived I have been surrounded by animals. They find me if I don't seek them. My collection really flourished after I moved into the cottage on the Durham/Yorkshire border. My Dad was raised only a few miles from there and I feel very much at home. I was never really at ease living in a town, and people object to noisy animals. It didn't seem to matter that I objected to noisy people! I regularly subscribed to the rural weekly newspapers and eventually spotted the ad I was waiting for: 'Isolated country cottage, needs attention', etc. By now I was used to the jargonese and could translate that as 'derelict', but that would be the only sort of property I could afford.

Fortunately for me it was the middle of a very severe winter and I knew that would put off a lot of other potential buyers. To view the cottage I followed in the wake of a snow plough. The drifts were twelve feet deep up the lane. I didn't need the key – I walked in through the window. It was a surveyor's dream. Everything that could be wrong, was. Dry rot, wet rot, rising damp, broken chimneys, smashed roof tiles, broken windows . . . I loved it. I've always been able to see potential in things, and this cottage cried out to be lived in and loved again. Many months of hard labour went into making it home; good friends showed their true worth as they happily spent weekends mixing concrete and stripping walls. It is now home to more than sixty living souls, with the garden hardly usable as every square foot has some sort of animal enclosure built on it.

January

'It's happening again!' I screamed down the garden. Malcolm, my long suffering husband, played his award-winning performance of being deaf yet again. It is a habit you develop when surrounded by screaming parrots. 'These rotten rubber gloves are freezing to the dishes – I am spilling everything.' At this point I have to say that I am not a winter person. I am a Leo and a true sun child and I don't like the cold. Animal keepers are unanimous in agreeing that winter can be hell.

There I was bravely battling through the snow dressed in most of my winter wardrobe. I have been known to wear four sweaters at once, even though it is a bit restricting and I usually look like a demented Michelin tyre man. Only two hundred yards away is a door leading to heaven, but I can't go in yet. Well, it's my idea of heaven on a freezing day – a log fire blazing up the chimney and a comfy chair, to be shared with a couple of cats and a dog, if he can squeeze on.

As usual, I am digressing. Let me explain about the gloves. In the winter, I always wear woollen gloves and then rubber gloves on top. In theory, that stops my hands getting wet. (Fashion experts, take note.) I'll do anything to protect my puny extremities. So from head to toe, I look like a mobile jumble sale. The cottage is on a slight rise, the Durham/Yorkshire border area is not exactly famous for its balmy climate – and unfortunately feeding animals is a three hundred and sixty-five days a year job.

A large part of my animal collection is made up of parrots. Because they have very destructive beaks, the food and water dishes are made of galvanised metal. As soon as the frost bites I shiver and spill everything; in the Arctic North, the water freezes instantly and there I am stuck to the dish again. With this problem in mind, I have been working on an invention to stop the water freezing. After three disasters, I think I have got it right and I'll be launching it to the long-suffering bird fanciers at the next National Exhibition of Cage and Aviary Birds. You can call me Heath, we'll forget about the formalities! But this particular winter, I was still doing my daily Charlie Chaplin routine of the dish sticking to one

2

hand, me pulling it off and it sticking to the other hand, and so on, and so on . . .

I am not the only creature in the cottage who hates the winter. ET, the nearly bald blue and yellow macaw, is definitely of like mind. Along with the four cats and three dogs, she is happy to hog the space in front of the fire or around the nearest radiator. It may sound strange, as traditionally cats and birds are bitter enemies, but there's always been a truce declared between them all. Mainly, I think, because the cats rapidly found out that there is no messing with this macaw. If you have a go she bites back.

She is totally mental and knows absolutely no fear. She looks like a chicken that is just about to be put in the oven. Before I got her she suffered terribly from stress and consequently developed the dreadful habit of plucking out her feathers. Like nail biting in humans, it seems that once birds start this they can very rarely be made to give up and so ET looks absolutely appalling. She is not like the normal picture you have of a macaw. You know, the beautiful blue and gold feathers, the very long tail and the magnificent aura: the traditional image the uninitiated have of parrots. She is quite naked in all the parts of her body she can reach with her lethal beak. She is capable of flying but she doesn't seem inclined to, probably because of the mess she has made of her feathers. She walks everywhere. In fact she waddles like ET, which is the reason I gave her that name.

In the summer she spends a lot of her time waddling around the garden, but in the winter she lives indoors because being half naked she really can't cope with the climate in the north of England. She very rapidly discovered that she didn't have to stay on the stand she was put on, but could find ways of clambering down. It is quite a ridiculous thing to watch, a bird that has the power of flight teetering on the edge of a perch and trying to catch hold of something with her beak to lower herself down. She quickly found out that if she got off the stand and on to the window seat, walked along the window seat and got on to the sofa, she could easily get on to the floor, and once on the floor, of course, the world is her oyster.

Parrots are very intelligent and with intelligence comes

curiosity. ET is no exception. Rapidly into everything that she shouldn't be. I've got a large open fireplace that burns logs. It is very black and sooty and it took ET no time at all to discover that it was quite amusing to head off towards it. She knows perfectly well she is not supposed to. As soon as I tell her not to, it's a game, a matter of how quickly she can get in there before I can catch her.

She has also developed a way of getting fed before everyone else. I'm not really sure how she discovered this; probably, like many great discoveries of our time, it was an accident. She was pottering about the kitchen one day – she tends to follow me about, as though she were attached by a piece of elastic to one of my shoes. I've often stood on her tail and accidentally pulled a tail feather out, because I turn round and she is just standing there, particularly when it is feeding time and I'm cutting up all the food to give to the other birds. You know how you see commandos going fist over fist up a rope – well, she uses my trousers going beak over foot up my leg until she can climb on to the working surface. Then she proceeds to help herself to any tasty morsel she fancies. I keep putting her back down, but in the end it gets to be a waste of time because you spend more time putting the macaw down on the floor than you do cutting up the food. She usually ends up getting her own way.

One day I didn't have jeans on for a change (that's normally part of my uniform: I think most people think I was born in jeans), I had bare legs. I was standing in my dressing gown one morning and I wasn't best pleased about ET's attempts to climb up my leg, because a macaw's beak digging in your thigh at any time of the day is no joy. I was being very, very insistent that she wasn't going to get up on to the working surface that morning. So, she decided to try and climb up the fridge door. Macaw's beaks are quite big, so she could put her beak round into the lip of the door where the rubber seal is, but she swung just that little bit too much on the fridge door and it opened. It took her no time at all to discover how to repeat this process and, of course, the fridge is an Aladdin's cave, full of goodies. No intelligent bird worth its salt could fail to get back in there and investigate.

One day I came home to find everything out of the fridge and spread all over the kitchen floor. The cats were sitting licking their lips, finishing off the prawns and paddling in spilt milk. I cleaned it all up and played hell with the cats, but I wasn't really sure who was responsible. In those cases I scream at everybody and hope that the culprit feels guilty enough not to do it again.

A couple of days after that, I was in one of the rooms off the living room and I heard ET going through her whole performance of swinging down and getting off her stand. I peeped through the half-opened door, and watched what happened. She clambered from the stand and headed off into the kitchen. I waited until she was through the kitchen door and then I tiptoed after her. Just as she reached the fridge and put her beak around the edge of the door, I coughed and she froze. It was an absolutely classic 'It's not me, nothing to do with me, I wasn't near the fridge, didn't even touch it, honest.' She just turned round and walked back into the living room as though nothing had happened. It is so difficult at times like that not to laugh. You try to be the stern disciplinarian, but it just looked so hysterical. This ridiculous, half-bald macaw waddling across the floor, deserving to be nominated for the next Oscar for her performance as the totally innocent, misunderstood creature. She came back and climbed back on to her stand nice as you please.

The following day I was outside looking in through the kitchen window, watching all the cats and the macaw just messing about in the living room. They play together on the floor, a ridiculous game of tig off the ground: one of them runs and another one jumps on the settee and the other one runs after it. Absolute mayhem but quite harmless in itself. I let them get on with it. As usual when I start watching I cannot stop. This is half the thing about keeping animals, you get so much pleasure from just watching their antics on a day to day basis and you learn the most amazing things quite out of the blue.

Eventually the cats got tired and they all went and spread

out in their usual favourite places: Tucker behind the sofa, Leo and Lucy on the window seat and Black Puss stretched across the fireplace. The macaw decided to go and investigate the fridge. Now, what was fascinating about this was how one animal can learn from another so quickly, and their actions can be triggered by certain things. Anyone who owns a dog or cat and feeds it on tinned food will know that the second you start to open a tin, that animal will appear from absolutely nowhere and be sitting adoringly at your side. You can be opening a tin of anything at any time of the day or night: they will hear the tin opener and it is a trigger. They're there and waiting. This little episode was a bit like that. The moment the macaw went into the kitchen, her claws started to make a click, click, click noise on the hard floor. As soon as she had done three paces the cats, as one body, woke up and ran to the kitchen door. I couldn't believe my eyes as I watched the cavalcade proceed down the kitchen; macaw first, Leo, who is the boss cat, next, then Lucy, Black Puss and Tucker in a line. Click, click, click, they headed towards the fridge. The cats sat down making a semi-circular audience, awaiting the macaw's great trick of the day. ET clipped her beak round the fridge, into the rubber seal, swung with all her might and the fridge door opened. She then stood back and looked at the cats, virtually waiting for a round of applause.

Of course, the cats weren't going to give her any credit at all at this point. Get in the fridge quick while you can before *she* comes back, was their attitude. They were in the fridge, paws out, poking around seeing what they could scoop up. The macaw just sat there and watched them. I was gaping at them through the window and again I coughed. The cats and the macaw flew off in every direction. By the time I got back into the house, the cats were all sitting in their proper places, the macaw was wandering around the living room floor and it so happened that the fridge door was just a little bit open but it wasn't us, honest.

With constant chaos in the cottage, you would expect the place to resemble the aftermath of the Harrods sale, but thanks to Mrs Dent, everything is remarkably clean and in order. Mrs Dent is our lovely lady 'what does'. Fortunately all the animals adore her. Can you imagine trying to clean windows with a macaw sitting on the edge of the bucket and throwing the chammy leather out at every chance she gets? Even Mrs Dent's patience is sometimes strained and ET gets an impromptu bath in whatever soapy substance is in the bucket at the time. But ET is not a bird to hold grudges and she continues to be seen wandering around after Mrs Dent like a distorted shadow.

January is a reasonably quiet month in the animal world, despite what I've told you so far. There's no breeding going on and no young injured birds to take care of. Generally it's a time for getting ready for the next breeding season. The best bit is preparing the nesting boxes. I always find this exciting. They say don't count your chickens etc, but I can't help counting the parrots, it's such a thrilling moment when you peek in and see that first egg. Parrots can be very destructive and some nest boxes have to be held together with six-inch nails and a prayer by the end of the season. Cockatoos are the worst. Molly and Freddie can make match-wood out of a three-quarter inch thick wooden nest box in under a week. It's so frustrating – all man's ingenuity goes into assisting the reproduction of these dotty birds. On three occasions, Molly has laid eggs only to deposit herself, the eggs and a pile of wood shavings on the aviary floor. This works out as a very expensive omelette when cockatoo chicks can sell at £350 each. I must admit that I'd get pretty bored sitting on a couple of eggs in a tiny wooden room with a small window somewhere near the ceiling, with only my feathers to preen. At least I can doodle. But Molly's taken up wood carving. In some areas in the world, cockatoo breeders, in desperation, have taken to using galvanised dustbins as nest boxes. That's fine if you live in temperate Florida, but nights can be pretty cold even in the summer in my neck of the woods.

Although it's not a time for breeding in my collection, my neighbours' animals usually have other ideas. When you live in the country, January isn't January, it's the start of lambing. The townie's idea of the spring lamb frolicking is completely out of the window. The sooner they're born, the sooner they get fat and the sooner they go to market. It's not unusual

7

for me to pop down to see Marjorie, my nearest neighbour, in her lovely old farmhouse and find a lamb in the oven. No, not quite ready for the mint sauce, but a pathetic little bundle of fleece and feet! It will have just dropped into the world and into the snow and been quickly pushed into the Aga to revive it and let it know that the world isn't quite as unfriendly as first impressions would suggest.

I'm an absolute sucker for bottle-feeding these 'pet lambs'. Make no mistake here, 'pet lambs' is a bit of a misnomer. They are not destined to spend the next fifteen years being cossetted like the family dog. They are hand reared because they have been rejected by their mothers, but they are still potential Sunday lunches. Every year, there's always one tiny baby that looks as though it will never make it and Marjorie's husband, Douglas, always threatens me with emotional blackmail, saying, 'It won't last the night, if you don't take it.' Now I might seem crackers, but believe it or not, I've learned over the years to be at least a bit practical and I've always managed to say 'No.' It's not as cold-hearted as it sounds, because it didn't take me long to find out that Marjorie is just as soft as me and would always end up bottle-feeding the poor little bundle and staying up with it all night if necessary, just to make sure it survived. I could never be a farmer – I get too attached to everything. I've got ancient raggy hens waddling round on crutches: they wouldn't recognise an egg if they fell over one, and I couldn't eat them if I was starving.

Snow is always a problem and January brings its share. Apart from all the obvious factors, it's the weight of snow that's caused me to have one of my most uncomfortable nights. I always check all the animals last thing at night and one January night there was a lot of snow on the ground. It was a very clear moonlit night and very cold. One advantage of living in the country is that you see the night sky in all its splendour. In towns, street lighting makes star watching pretty difficult, but skies full of jewels are quite common over the cottage.

This particular night, despite the cold, our garden looked very beautiful with eerie moon shadows bouncing off the snow-covered aviaries. That is until I came to the owl aviary.

You know how it is when you expect to see something and it's not as it should be. You doubt whether your eyes are sending the right messages to your brain. So I stood there and did a double take to convince myself that I wasn't hallucinating. But I wasn't. The owl aviary had collapsed. Under normal circumstances, it is twelve feet long by six feet high by six feet wide and it contains five tawny owls, all retired with disability pensions. There's One Eye, who was in a fight with a sports car; Wattie and Edna, with two wings between them, courtesy of British Telecom; and Fluff and Squeak, who've got all their bits but don't quite function well. On this occasion, I didn't expect to see any of my feathered friends left. They say 'the wise old owl' and I reckon this bunch are pretty smart, because despite the fact that the whole aviary had collapsed around them, they were all still sitting on their usual perches, at least bits of the perches that remained.

What had happened was the wind had been so strong that snow had drifted from the adjoining goat house on to the aviary roof and the weight had caused the whole structure to cave in. As this had happened, the two six foot square back panels of the aviary had been whipped away by the wind and were fifteen yards down the field. The wire netting at the front had been pulled away from the retaining base; it had coiled back up like a spring and deposited the snow in small mounds so that the aviary looked like an alpine model village with Wattie and Co all perched on top. I don't know if you have ever seen a mime artiste doing a 'walking against the wind' routine, but that was me at 11 p.m., in a ploughed field, trying to get a six foot square panel back in position. The one good thing about living in the middle of nowhere is you can swear like mad really loud without offending anyone. Mind, there's always the chance that the odd smart parrot might pick up a bit of extra fruity vocabulary and save it for the day you're showing the Lady Mayoress around the garden.

Another good point about country life is everybody mucks in and at 11 p.m., I wouldn't think twice about phoning my neighbours and dragging them away from a cosy fireplace to come and help, because I'd expect them to do the same to me.

The tawny owl is one of our most popular native birds and one of my favourites. I've looked after dozens of these beautiful birds over the last few years and each one has had a different personality.

The five residents all live active lives, but for various reasons are unable to be released. The owl is the silent hunter – the farmer's friend, ridding the fields and the farmyards of many of his enemies. Farms are about economy and we may feel that one small rat, or one even smaller mouse, doesn't do that much damage. Multiply this by hundreds and consider how frequently they are capable of reproducing and a great deal of the farmer's crop can disappear, long before harvest time.

Because owls need to hunt, they must be able to fly with supreme efficiency and their wings must be in perfect order. And as with all birds of prey, it is the feet and talons, and not the beak, that are the real killers, and they too must be in perfect working order. To release an owl, without all his faculties, would certainly mean condemning him to death by starvation.

The most endearing owl that I have today is the one I call Wattie. He was brought to me by a passing motorist after he'd lost a wing flying into a telegraph wire. If you've ever had the opportunity to be close to a tawny owl, you'll almost certainly remember his greeting. The rapid clacking noise he makes with his beak to warn you of his presence is like the sound that children make when they pretend to be cowboys and Indians, and ride an imaginary horse with one hand flailing the wind, to increase the speed of their imaginary steed. This sound is also reminiscent of someone who has a bit of a problem with loose false teeth, and that is how Wattie was christened.

One of the more colourful characters of the village was a man known to us all simply as Wattie. Wattie had his own stool in the corner of the bar in the village pub and would take nightly residence and several drinks and preside over the evening's comings and goings. He had a big, red, shiny, well-scrubbed face. He had spent most of his life outdoors and you knew that at night when he took off his clothes to go to bed, his magnificent tan would end at his collar line and start again just below the elbows. Wattie had difficulty in communicating and preceded every sentence with a rapid succession of clicks, emanating from his loose fitting teeth. The proportion of clicks to speech grew greater as the evening wore on and the alchohol consumption went up. Wattie's wife was named Edna and so naturally the next owl that came into my care, at this time, was duly christened Edna.

Edna arrived in a sorry state. She had obviously been on her maiden flight without much success and arrived with a badly broken wing. It was so bad that amputation was the only answer. They make a fine pair, just like bookends. They have remained devoted to each other since they first met. However Wattie, just like his human counterpart, is much more extrovert than Edna. To this day, if you go to the owl aviary at any time of the day you may only see one of the owls. You can guarantee it is Wattie. He'll be on his favourite perch and will whizz his head round to look you full in the eye and say hello. Or, if you speak Wattie, *clack, clack, clack, clack.*

February

. . . Still bloody freezing. Note the meteorological terminology!

One thing I could never do is make a living out of breeding animals. I am just far too fussy about the homes that they'll go to after mine. On the rare occasion that I've sold a parrot, it feels like giving a baby up for adoption. I always demand full visiting rights and regular progress reports. With this in mind and the fact that I spend a fortune every week on taking care of animals, I've got to have a regular income.

The best job, time wise, that I've ever had as far as animal keeping is concerned, was at Tyne Tees Television, presenting the weather and doing animal-related items for a programme called *Northern Life*. This was an early evening news magazine programme and I didn't start work until 3 p.m. and was finished by 7 p.m. It was great! It meant I could spend the best part of my day with the animals and then pop off up the motorway to Newcastle and earn the money to continue my chosen lifestyle.

While I was working there, I got involved in a talking bird competition . . . This is the sort of event that is used by editors to fill a gap in what is known as the silly season. Little which is newsworthy happens in the doldrum period after Christmas, so TV and newspapers alike come up with oddities to fill time and space and keep the public amused. Things so often amuse me when working with animals. There are so many incidents that just make you laugh out loud, particularly with people and their animals. The people are trying to impress, but animals are like children: they let you down terribly, they are so honest. They reveal all your hidden secrets. You know, if you've got a secret box of chocolates tucked away and you're supposed to be on a diet, you can be damn sure that when somebody comes in and you have just convinced them you've lost half a stone and you haven't eaten a thing all day, the dog will go and stick his nose in the hidden box of chocolates and give away your secret . . . This competition was an ideal example.

The north's best talking bird came from the Tyne Tees area and it was a budgie called Sparky. There are recordings of Sparky saying hundreds of different words; he had a phenomenal vocabulary for such a tiny bird. Anyway,

Sparky had died and in his honour we had decided to run a contest to search for Sparky Mark II in the Tyne Tees Television area. I had been sent off to the local art college where they were making a wonderful Sparky Trophy out of crystal, a replica of Sparky himself. I watched the trophy being made and reported on it on film for the programme, using that to trail the competition. For the competition itself, we invited people from all over the region to enter their talking birds. We didn't want people to travel from each corner of the region to bring their birds to the studio, and we didn't fancy a studio full of birds either, so we decided that the best plan would be to set up heats in different hotels in the area. We met up with the people and their birds and we judged them, so that only the six finalists would be in the studio for the big night.

I went to hotels from the far reaches of Northumberland right down to York and met hundreds of people with their potential Sparky Mark II's. They had everything from budgies to mynah birds to parrots to cockatoos: all the traditional sorts of talking birds that you expect. All these people had arrived after sending in letters and photographs of their wonderful talking pets. We had tape recordings of them reciting nursery rhymes and the books of the Bible and prayers and absolutely everything you can think of. Potentially we had a great item on our hands. But as I said, animals let you down dreadfully. I had come up against dozens and dozens of birds at each hotel and I hardly got a squeak out of any of them. If they actually managed to say hello, that was it, they were in the final because we were getting desperate and of course the owners were too.

'Oh, when he's at home and I switch the light off he says goodnight and when I switch it on in the morning he says good morning and he asks for his tea and he calls my husband a silly bugger.' They were really mad at the birds. I felt sorry, really – when the birds got home they'd have hell to pay. Anyway, the last heat was in a hotel in Northumberland. I was absolutely desperate to find a bird that would say *something* because the night of the final was going to be fairly Spartan if all we had was one budgie that could manage to bash his bell in sequence with a ticking clock and another budgie that said, 'Get your knickers off.'

As soon as I arrived at this hotel, I noticed a magnificent medium sulphur crested cockatoo at the far end of the room. What was particularly good about this bird was that he wasn't in his cage, he was standing on it. From television's point of view it's much better if we can get a bird out of its cage, as it can be quite difficult for lighting purposes to shoot through the bars. We had been hoping for birds that would stand on people's shoulders or hands because at least we could see them. I decided there and then that even if it didn't say a word, if it had been mute from birth, this cockatoo would still be in the final, because at least we would have something worth looking at.

The producer spotted it at the same time as me and agreed totally. We went through the whole performance of going down the line of cages and people behaving absolutely ridiculously to the birds to try and make them talk. Some people will do anything to get on television and we began to wonder exactly who was mimicking whom. I had great visions of these budgies at home in their cages standing on their one leg, you know, looking at themselves in the mirror and saying 'Right, I'm going to get this silly sod at it again.' Just one chorus of 'who's a pretty boy then' and they're off. Their heads are in the cages and they'll look through the bars – 'Who's a pretty boy then, who's a pretty boy?' Quite hysterical to look at, but from the point of view of a talking bird competition we were absolutely snookered.

We hadn't got a thing and I was getting towards the end of the room where the cockatoo was and noticed that the owners of this particular bird were quite different from most of the others. They were two very, very camp men who were very theatrical. If the bird says nothing, I thought, at least we've got people who will talk and be amusing and these guys were absolutely outrageous. So that was another passport to the final for the cockatoo.

Obviously this cockatoo was a great performer, he was into showing off. Being the owner of a couple of cockatoos I know the signs straight away. One of the signs is that when a cockatoo is displaying and showing off, he erects the crest on the top of his head to its full extent, spreads his wings out and sort of bobs up and down. This one was already working before I got anywhere near the cage. I thought, 'Great, he's going to move, he looks good, the owners are a lot of fun, at least we have got something out of the day.'

The owners were standing up at either side of the cage and the cockatoo was still on the top. He stretched himself up to his full height, erected his crest, spread his wings bobbed his head forward, looked me straight in the eye and said, 'Who's a fucking poof then?' The place erupted. The owners started screaming, they thought it was outrageously wonderful, and the producer was ecstatic. Of course the cockatoo came to the studio and we were all praying that he would do a repeat performance because the programme was live, so there would be nothing we could do about it. It would certainly create a viewer reaction. The IBA could hardly go mad with us for a swearing cockatoo which was completely beyond our control and the ratings would have soared heavens high. But, as usual, when the cockatoo was in the studio on the night of the final, it didn't say a dickie bird. In fact I don't think any of them did.

On one of my many journeys to Newcastle, I met up with one of the most delightful birds I've ever had the privilege of spending some time with. It's strange, but when you are animal orientated, you notice things around you that a lot of people don't seem to see. I've often taken friends for a walk around the lanes surrounding my cottage and I am always amazed at how many things they don't see until they're pointed out to them. I once stopped a friend from standing on a hen pheasant sitting on her eggs on the grass verge just next to the hedgerow. I know pheasants are particularly well camouflaged, but as far as I was concerned, this one might as well have had a neon sign on her head – she was so obvious.

This particular day, when I was driving up the motorway, I saw what I thought was a hen pheasant pottering about on the hard shoulder. It's not uncommon in the winter months to see normally shy birds making an exhibition of themselves: hunger overcomes all the normal self-preservation tactics, including shyness. As I approached, this bird got closer and closer to the near side lane and the thunderous wheels of the massive trucks heading northwards to Scotland.

Someone once told me that some traffic research had been done which says that ten per cent more vehicles take the high road to Scotland than come back out on the low road back to the Sassenachs. I wonder what happens to them? All these stories about Nessie may have some foundation after all.

Now I know it's illegal to stop on the hard shoulder, and also pretty unsafe, but I never have been one to put life and limb – or the law, for that matter – before the welfare of an animal. My intention was to stop and shoo the silly bird back into the undergrowth on the motorway's edge. I stopped the car about twenty yards away from the bird, which was still furiously pecking at all those invisible things that birds seem to pick up on the roadside, and I seriously expected it to fly off as soon as I got out of the car. As a lot of wildlife photographers know, it's possible to get quite close to many animals and birds as long as you stay in the car. Once you're out of the car, you're instantly recognisable as that most dangerous of animals, the human, and the creature wisely makes a hasty retreat.

On this occasion, it didn't happen and I soon realised that what was ahead of me was not a hen pheasant, but a bird I had never encountered before. It was a hen. To be slightly more accurate, it was a bantam – and to be a hundred per cent accurate, it was a Poland bantam. Let me say at this point, that all this specific identification was with hindsight, the aid of several books and finally the worldly wisdom of my farmer neighbour. What I saw before me was a bird about the size of a good plump hen pheasant and about the same colour. She didn't have the long tail, but what she had at the other end more than made up for it. She looked as though she was wearing a hat. Not just any old hat, but a hat worthy of the Queen Mother on Ladies' Day at Royal Ascot. It started as a crown in the middle of her head, with black and brown speckled feathers fanning out in all directions, cascading all the way down to obsure the eyes totally. No wonder she was walking along so close to death.

17

She couldn't see a damn thing. Not only couldn't she see, but she must have been stone deaf. It was no problem at all for me to walk straight up to her, tuck her under my arm and take her back to the car.

I never found out how she came to be there, but over the following months, I was very glad that she was. Normally when I've collected injured birds from the roadside they flap about like mad and deposit small or sometimes large black and white presents all over me and my car in gratitude for my valiant rescue. This one sat on the front seat; the second I turned the car engine on she nestled down as though she was incubating a clutch of the most precious eggs and didn't move until I arrived in Newcastle. She didn't even leave a deposit.

The headdress she was wearing resembled a bedraggled feather duster and I immediately christened her Moppet. When I arrived at Tyne Tees, the security man, who was always very interested in all the animals I took to the studio, immediately got a bowl of water and carried it up to my dressing room, where Moppet had already made herself very much at home. He then dashed off to the canteen to scrounge a few tasty morsels to keep her going. When he came back to the dressing room, he reminded me in true security man's fashion to make sure that I kept my dressing room door locked. He remembered the last time I had a bird in my dressing room.

I'd taken a New Zealand parakeet called a Kakariki in for a programme on endangered species. These delightful little green birds, not much larger than budgies, are becoming extremely rare in their native habitat but many keen bird fanciers have found them relatively easy to breed in captivity. At this time I had seven pairs and the hens have been known to lay ten eggs at one time. I never understand how such a tiny bottom can manage to keep all these eggs at a temperature of just over 98° Farenheit, which is needed to hatch them successfully. However, it did and I was taking one of these babies to the studio to illustrate the importance of captive breeding as a conservation measure.

I put the cage in my dressing room and was filling up the water dish. In the split second that the dish was removed, the kakariki took its chance and flew out of the hole left in the side of the cage where the dish had been. My dressing room door was open and out flew the bird. I followed swiftly behind, just in time to see it disappearing up through the open loft door and into the roof of the studio building.

Birds instinctively fly upwards when frightened and despite the fact that it was dark, the loft must have looked like the best route to freedom. Under normal circumstances, the loft would have been closed, but the electricians were doing some rewiring and had gone off to take the statutory tea break and left the door open. Now I'm terrified of heights, but I had to do something.

On my way up to the dressing rooms that day, I'd noticed some decorators working in one of the corridors, so I ran to ask them if I could borrow a ladder. So many bizarre things have happened to me in the past with animals and television studios that they weren't unduly surprised at my request. One of the men, being a true warmhearted Geordie, offered to help. I must admit I was secretly relieved, as I was not looking forward to crawling round a dark loft, trying to catch a tiny frightened parakeet all on my own. We positioned the ladder under the hole and my Sir Galahad ascended the ladder in his shining armour, well disguised as a white painter's overall. It wasn't long before I heard a muffled, 'Bloody hell, it's like the black 'ole of Calcutta up 'ere!' and then a more distinct, 'I'm sorry pet, but I can't seem to see it.' At this point I was getting quite worried for the safety of the bird and I ran down to security to get a couple of torches.

The very same security man who later helped me with Moppet returned with me and immediately went into the role of being in charge (it's funny what a uniform does to a person), screaming instructions to the by now demented decorator. They eventually spotted the bird perched on one of the cross beams and – you've guessed it – in the farthest corner away from the loft hole.

Studio lofts are just the same as normal house lofts, in as much as to cross from one side to the other, you've got to balance on the beams placed just over a foot apart. It's difficult enough if you just want to move from one side to the other, but to catch a bird as well, it seemed nigh on impossible. To add to the problems, there were lots of loose wires lying around, left by the electricians, who were sat in the canteen blissfully unaware of the chaos we were causing to their neatly arranged cables. Fred, the painter – by now we were on intimate terms – was doing his very best. Apart from the darkness, the impossibility of movement, the likelihood of strangulation or an electric shock, he was also sweating profusely because the temperature in the loft was not unlike that of a sauna. Between us we decided it would be best to approach the bird by keeping a low profile, so Fred set off on hands and knees, crawling across the beams, while the security man and I held our breath.

The master plan was that Fred would try and shoo the bird towards the loft hole and we hoped that it would be attracted by the light and fly back down into the corridor, where I would be waiting to shoo it back towards the open dressing room door. The first part of the plan worked like a dream – apart from poor Fred's obvious discomfort – but as usual, it's difficult to predict the movements of any animal accurately, particularly a frightened one. The kakariki flew towards the loft hole, but totally ignored it; she continued on to the other extremity of the loft and resettled in the same position on the diagonally opposite cross beam. It was plain this wasn't going to work. Plan B had to be thought of and quickly.

We would have to get something to catch the bird in – Fred came down the ladder. By this time he was bent double, beetroot red and rubbing his knees. But in true knight in shining armour style, he didn't complain and seemed quite keen to continue the conquest. We went back to the other decorator – who was still painting the same piece of wall, oblivious to all around him – and asked if we could borrow one of the large dust sheets he was using to protect the carpet. He was more than pleased to oblige, as that seemed like a good enough excuse for him to stop work. We returned with the dust sheet and fearless Fred went back up into the hell hole. It was six or seven fly pasts later that the now very tired little bird was bagged under the dust sheet. Fred descended triumphantly and apart from being very dirty, the bird seemed to have suffered no ill effects. I couldn't say the same for Fred. I don't think he'll ever be the same again. But what really worried Fred was how was he going to explain to his wife where he'd got all the bruises on his knees from. I said to tell her the truth and explain what'd happened and he said, 'Would you believe it!?'

As soon as I realised that the bird was OK, I popped out of the studios, ran to the off-licence and bought half a dozen cans of the nectar of Newcastle – brown ale. Fred was greatly appreciative, but did suggest that if he arrived home pissed, as well as having bruised knees, he'd have no chance with the wife.

Needless to say, I was not going to make the same mistake twice. Moppet behaved impeccably in my dressing room. On the journey back to the cottage, she reacted in the same unaffected way and sat on the front seat of the car as if it was a thing that she did every day of her life. She was undoubtedly the tamest hen that I have ever encountered and rewarded me for her rescue the very next morning by laying a lovely brown egg. I never found out where Moppet came from. I was quite pleased about that, because it would have been very hard to give her back. She lived happily with us for a couple of years, laying vast quantities of eggs and tootling around the garden with her silly hat on, looking absolutely hysterical after it had rained.

One night when I went to lock in the hens, Moppet wasn't there. I always hate this, because of course I think of all the dreadful things that could happen and Moppet, in particular, was so tame and couldn't see danger if it came up and hit her on the beak.

The next day, the worst was confirmed. About ten yards from the back garden, in the field next door, I found a pile of Moppet feathers. At first I blamed a fox. Bantams have annoying habits and when they decide to get broody, they object to you removing their eggs. If you don't leave them one to sit on, they'll go off and secretly deposit the eggs somewhere else. The night they don't come home, you know they've decided they've laid enough to make it worthwhile sitting on them and so they stay in the secret hiding hole. I was sure this was what Moppet had done and I searched up and down the hedgerow for the nest.

It wasn't until several weeks later that I found out where the nest was – it was the day that Rags, the Airedale cross, his name says it all, came back into the cottage, stinking to high heaven of the fragrant odour reminiscent of a school playground, after the boys had been to the joke shop. The smell of rotten eggs is only surpassed, in my opinion, by the smell of rotten fish. Rags had discovered the five eggs on one of his many attempts to escape from the garden by uprooting one of the hedges. With dogs' noses being as sensitive as they are, it must have been a dreadful shock to him, to be suddenly covered by this rotten gooey mess, but it certainly worked as a deterrent. He didn't try to get out of the garden for quite some time after that. The only problem was, I couldn't stand him in the house either. It took ages to bath away that stink, but with a combination of Dettol, washing up liquid and finally, in desperation, Chanel No 5 Bubble Bath, he became almost bearable.

It was many months later that I discovered the truth about Moppet's demise. My neighbour's son overheard a couple of well-known poachers talking in the village pub – one telling the other about how his lurcher dog had decided to be lazy one day and had not bothered running after the hare but had bagged one of Wincey Willis's funny-looking chickens instead. All I can say is it's a good job I wasn't in the pub at the time, or they would have been wearing the beer instead of drinking it.

March

I like March. Despite the fact that the weather isn't all that fabulous, we do get occasional sneak previews of spring, even in the north. There are always a lot of crocuses about, you can see the buds starting to swell on the trees and some of the early breeding parrots are already sitting on eggs. It's also quite traumatic because the severe variations in temperature and particularly the long night-time frosts can cause a lot of heartache when eggs fail to hatch. Even though at times conditions have been dreadful, my oldest pair of Alexandrines have never let me down.

The hen is an excellent mother and once her three precious eggs have been laid, she hardly leaves the nest box. Dad proudly sits on guard in the outside flight, warning everyone and everything to stay well clear of his territory. He is an ideal husband and attends to all mother's needs, making sure she is regularly fed and, at night, climbing into the nest box to sit alongside his wife and keep her and their future offspring safe and warm. I bought the hen in the hot summer of 1976. If you'd seen her then, you would swear it couldn't possibly be the same bird now.

At that time I was working as a record plugger touring a territory that stretched from Sheffield in the south to Glasgow and Edinburgh in the north and Belfast in the west. My job was to call on television and radio stations and one or two of the more important record stores, 'important' ones being those which were used to compile the record charts. Each time they sold a record it was ticked on a list. These ticks were totalled up and the chart places were worked out from the sales figures. It was an old dodge to give lots of free records to the dealer. He would then sell them at one hundred per cent profit and we would get the precious ticks. A lot of dubious chart places resulted from this practice. Since those days a severe shake-up has occurred and a new system is in operation. But wherever I was, I always took the chance to find the local pet shops.

One day when the temperature was in the 80's, I called into a pet shop that I'd been told about. The first thing I saw was a panting, dehydrated green Alexandrine parrot. Its feathers were brittle and there was no sign of water in the cage at all. Yet again I cursed the inadequacy of the inspec-

24

tion procedure laid down in this country to govern the issue of trading licences to pet shop owners. It's always infuriated me that many of these inspectors seem more concerned about a crack in a lavatory seat than the condition in which the livestock is held. They seem to be about as qualified to check on animal welfare as I would be to teach higher mathematics at Oxford.

Apart from the lack of water, this pathetic creature was standing on a perch nearly half an inch thick with grease and with three or four inches of excrement on the cage floor. This breed of bird has a long tail and the cage being far too small meant that the tail feathers were thickly encrusted with dirt as they dragged along the bottom of the cage. Its eyes were dull and I was sure it was not long for this world. At times like this, I'm always racked with an overpowering desire to save the bird but I know that spending money in this sort of establishment encourages the trade to continue. I also find it extremely difficult to keep my temper with the pet shop owner. I've probably been thrown out of more pet shops than a Chelsea football supporter has been thrown out of pubs on a Saturday.

There was no way that I could go home and sleep well that night leaving the parrot to its fate. I gritted my teeth and asked the price. I explained that as I had come unprepared to buy a bird, I would need to borrow a cage to take it home in. The cage in which the parrot was currently incarcerated was absolutely disgusting. Apart from the fact that it had evidently not been cleaned for months, it was also rotten and rusty. The pet shop owner said that I could take the bird in the cage, but must promise to return it immediately as he would need it for future stock. I said very little. I paid up and left the shop, without the slightest intention of ever returning this heap of scrap metal to inflict on the next unfortunate resident. I did in fact dump it at a local tip as I was too ashamed to leave it for the dustmen in case they thought for one minute that I'd ever kept any bird in it.

After two months in an aviary with good food and bathing facilities, the bird was displaying her true glory with bright green shiny feathers, a bright red shiny beak and a twinkle in her eye.

Not long after this, I got a phone call from my mother to say that an old man in her street had asked if I wanted his parrot. It had been his wife's pet and she had died. Apart from the obvious distressing association with the bird and his wife, he admitted that he really couldn't be bothered to take care of it properly. People who are not keen bird lovers tend to class all parrots together and this man could not tell me on the phone what kind of bird it was. When I went to collect it, I was really chuffed to find that it was a cock Alexandrine – just what I'd been looking for. He too was in a pretty poor state. His cage was far too small and since his owner's death, he'd been confined in it. There was not even enough room for him to stretch his wings and he was dry, bedraggled and dirty.

I like playing Cupid. It's a magic moment when you introduce two birds who have lived in isolation for so long – parrots pair for life and spend a lot of time preening each other and generally interacting. It was love at first sight and since then, they have been responsible for the arrival of fifteen new Alexandrines into the world. They are both still going strong and I hope they will continue to do so for many years to come.

Another reason why March is one of my more favourite months is that it's tortoise time. I always bring my tortoises out of hibernation in March, whatever the weather outside. In their natural habitat, tortoises would enjoy a much longer summer than we have to suffer in the British Isles. When I keep any wild animal in captivity I feel it's my responsibility to duplicate as nearly as possible the conditions in which they would normally live. For this reason, one of my first priorities on moving into the cottage was to establish an animal room with heat lamps, humidity controllers and time switches to regulate the length of simulated daylight hours.

The tortoises spend the first couple of months after hibernation in this room and are only allowed out into their enclosure in the garden when there is enough sunshine around to give them the heat they need to function properly. I am always excited when they slowly warm up and open their eyes after such a long sleep. I never fail to be impressed by the miracle of hibernation and, with my natural distaste for cold weather, I'm a little bit envious of the tortoises' facility to go to sleep and ignore the whole thing. They're always given a shallow, warm bath and then a massage to help encourage the blood flow back through their little stiff, cold limbs.

I've got one male tortoise who is the randiest thing on four legs. Don't ever let anyone tell you that a tortoise is slow. He seems to spend the whole hibernation period recuperating his strength for the orgy to come. As soon as he's warm through, he has a quick drink and then he's off like a rocket in search of any unwary female tortoise who may still be drowsy from her long sleep. He's like a stag at rutting time. Within the first couple of days, he's re-established his conjugal rights with the whole collection. His sexuality has sometimes been in question as he has spent many long afternoons making advances to other male tortoises in the group and once I even caught him attempting to mate with half a rubber ball that one of the dogs had left lying in the garden. I don't know when he ever gets the time to eat, as it often seems that from first light to dusk, he spends the whole day bonking round the garden. If you've never witnessed a tortoise at stud, it is one of nature's more amusing sights. It starts with foreplay, but certainly not the kind that would do very much for me: the male attempts to bite any extremity that's sticking out of his lady love's shell. This can often end in a tortoise receiving quite serious injuries. I've actually seen one tortoise, who was extremely frustrated by the lack of effect his courtship was having on his chosen female, rolling the female over and over and over along the garden until she must have been so dizzy that she couldn't run away. While she was immobile Casanova mounted from behind and proceeded round the garden in piggyback fashion, his mouth wide open, letting out a peculiar little noise every time he attempted to thrust his point home. With that kind of vicious foreplay, it wouldn't surprise me if a lot of female tortoises also get headaches.

Animal lovers come in all shapes and sizes, and it's always a great source of entertainment for me to visit one of the many animal symposiums held around the country. March usually sees me heading down to Bristol for the annual symposium at Bristol University, organised by the British Chelonia Group. This group consists of tortoise fanatics from all over the UK. It was founded to advance people's knowledge of the welfare, conservation and care in captivity of tortoises, terrapins and turtles. They have done some marvellous work and I try never to miss the annual meeting of like minds. Everyone has something to contribute, from professors to enthusiastic amateurs. Many a keen amateur has discovered a new fact about their much loved pet, by close and caring observation, where the same information has evaded the analytical gaze of the scientist.

It's not only reptile keepers that come in varying guises. I remember once being called to the reception at Tyne Tees Television. I was told by the lady on the phone that a stinking tramp insisted on seeing me and she thought that he had something live stuffed underneath his raggy overcoat. I ran down the stairs to be met by truly the smelliest person I'd ever seen. I was sure that he had something live underneath his overcoat. In fact several things – fleas, lice, you name it. I went as close as I could bear and he opened his overcoat to reveal a young herring gull. Even a young herring gull is not small and it has a pretty vicious bite, but he'd managed to secrete it about his person without receiving a serious injury – I suspect the gull had been overcome by the smell and was too weak to resist. It transpired that this tramp had risked life and limb to rescue the gull from the railway line in the newly built Metro station. It had flown into an overhead wire and dropped on to the track. Its wing was quite badly damaged and it had lost a lot of feathers. By the time I'd got it home, both of us needed delousing! I kept it for two years while it moulted out into more and more adult plumage and underwent a successful operation to repair the wing. When the day of release came, I wished I'd been able to contact the tramp and let him know his effort had been worthwhile.

On the rare occasions when neither Malcolm nor myself can be at the cottage, our very dear friend Philip moves in to take charge. Philip Dale has been a friend for many years. We met when I was working with a friend of his at Radio Tees. At that time Philip had a twenty-eight inch waist and was one of the best dancers I'd ever seen. During the years I've known him, he has learnt ice skating and been brilliant, learnt tennis and been brilliant. He's also taken up acting, at which he excels, but the thing he's done best of all is to put on weight! I've never known anyone gain and lose weight as he can. When he's eating it's as though he's training to eat for Britain in the next Olympics – 'double chips, fish, peas and a sausage please, to tide me over till we get home.' When he's dieting, he'll live for days on a lettuce leaf. At the moment he's in training, so picture a russet-haired man, of ample proportions (I'm being kind now cos I want him to look after the animals again), 5' 8" with large brown eyes. Philip has very pale skin and likes to lie around indoors all day. Whatever possessed him to agree to look after the animals is beyond me. On paper he would hardly seem ideally suited. I suppose that's the measure of a true friend.

The first time he agreed to take on this awesome responsibility, I spent a couple of days before I was due to go away going through the routine with him and leaving copious notes on feeding and the do's and don'ts of taking care of such a motley collection. With so much to teach him in such a short time, it was almost certain that I'd forget something. One of the more exotic members of the Willis household was a three-quarters grown green iguana. She lived in a huge vivarium in one corner of the living room and was responsible for inflicting many near heart attacks on trades people, such as the telephone engineer and the man who came to read the meter. In fact I'd had her from the hatching stage, with the result that she was very tame and rarely experienced fear – to her cost as I found out later.

Iguanas normally live in semi-tropical forest areas and are adept at climbing and swimming. In the wild, they are most often seen lying along branches overhanging water. This makes escape from danger easy and quick. When they're threatened in any way, they dive off the branch into the water, tucking their legs into their sides, and with a couple of thrashes of a very powerful tail, they speed through the water to safety.

In the vivarium I had arranged branches and a large container of water in an attempt to duplicate nature. I'd also installed a basking lamp to provide heat and a tru-lite tube, which simulates sunlight. The iguana spent much of the day soaking up the heat and rays. At night this light was switched off and the enclosure was allowed to cool down just as the night-time forest does.

Nature is truly marvellous in the way creatures evolve to suit their surroundings best. During the day, in the sunlight, an iguana takes on a bright green colour and disappears into the background of the lush, green foliage of its natural home. At night, as the forest cools and darkens, the iguana positions itself on a suitable branch where it slowly loses its bright green day dress and takes on sludgy browny grey pyjamas, equally effective as night-time camouflage.

Poor Philip knew nothing of this when he got up to face the rigours of the day that first morning. Ever conscious of the responsibility he'd taken on, and how I would feel if something went wrong, he was horrified when, dutifully following my list of instructions, he switched on the iguana lights and saw the sleeping, almost comatose iguana.

Iguanas, like all reptiles, are cold blooded and need external heat to get them going for the day ahead, just as most of us need our first cup of coffee. Philip was convinced that this grey, limp animal was dead. He explained to me some time later that it was at this point that he discovered the real meaning of fear. He was sure that I would kill him when I got home and discovered that in one day he'd managed to kill off a creature that I'd been nurturing for five years. He proceeded to boost my phone bill by around fifty pounds by ringing every zoo and pet shop, including Harrods pet department, in a misguided attempt to replace the deceased. Of course, while he was doing this, time was passing and the heat was getting through. The telephone was on a shelf next to Iggy's cage. And just as he'd felt fear for the first time, he explained that he was also convinced he'd had his first heart attack, when the iguana, fully warmed through, jumped off the branch to go and have a drink. It constantly amazes me that after such a baptism of fire, Philip still returns and takes over whenever he is asked.

It's not unusual to encounter a variety of animals in all corners of the cottage. I can never understand people who buy a dog and leave it out in a kennel in the garden. Surely the joy of owning an animal is increased tenfold when you share your life with it. Sometimes people say we do go a bit far, but on one occasion, I could see no other choice than to bring the goat to live in the house for a while.

Didi is an African pygmy goat and as a kid, she was a star in one of the animal programmes I did for Granada Television. She is about the size of a large dog, very stocky and with beautiful black and white markings. She also has a lethal pair of horns and a temperament to match.

One morning, I went to the top of the garden as usual to let Didi into her enclosure, but she didn't make any attempt to move let alone go through our normal routine of mock fighting. I immediately rang the vet and as usual Neville came hot foot from the surgery.

Neville is a wonderful person. I've always been a bit in awe of vets and the skills they possess. People have often asked me why I didn't become a vet. The simple answer is I'm just not brainy enough. Mathematics and the sciences leave me cold, but what I have got is instinct. Instinct with animals and instinct with people. I usually make rapid character assessments and I've rarely been wrong.

There was one occasion when I didn't get it quite right, and I should have listened to what the animals were trying to tell me. I had a chap round to redo the roof on the cottage. The back of the cottage has got a very low sloping roof – it faces west and there is a prevailing westerly wind. Obviously over the years the wind has worn away at the roof quite heavily and we were getting a bit of seepage. This chap came to give me an estimate on a new kind of treatment to put on it. He seemed all right when I met him. But when he came into the house the dogs went completely crackers and all the time that he was there they were growling and grumpy. It was obvious that they just didn't like him. He seemed to know what he was talking about and gave us a reasonable estimate, so he came back and did the work and the dogs were right. Within three months the roof was leaking again, the man had disappeared off the face of the earth and I was £500 out of pocket. So I trust the instincts of my animals and go along with them. They undoubtedly have an ability to suss people out. Perhaps better than people can.

From the first day I met Neville, I liked and admired him. He's a tall, smiling-faced, attractive man with big, powerful but sensitive hands. He can tackle a rampant bull or repair the tiniest bird's wing. Being a country vet, he had had very little experience in dealing with anything more exotic than a cross-bred Charolet calf until I moved into the area. It didn't take him long to adapt his medical skills and my keeper's know-how into effective courses of treatment for anything I cared to present to him.

On this occasion he diagnosed a virus problem that normally affected sheep. The treatment, apart from medication, was that Didi must be kept warm and on no account be allowed to lie down on her side or she would rapidly develop pneumonia and die.

Neville was used to dealing with farmers and the economics rather than the sentimentality of animal welfare. He was used to diagnosing this problem with sheep, knowing only too well that it would condemn the sheep to the knacker's yard. Of course there was no chance of this with Didi. It was wholly impracticable for us to put heating into the goathouse and for one of us to spend the night and the other the whole day with her to make sure she didn't lie down. The cottage has always been cosy, but if you're looking for something out of *Ideal Home* magazine, then you've come to the wrong place. If we couldn't go to the goat, then the goat must come to us. The cottage is about one hundred and twenty-five years old, having started life as a two-roomed stone-built toll-gate house. Over the years many extensions have been added in all different directions and I doubt if its original owner would recognise it if he could return today.

In the centre of the cottage, there's a small passageway, leading from the living room, past the bathroom and one of the bedrooms, into what is now the animal room. This passageway has a stone floor under the carpet and since we moved in, it also has a radiator. We took up the carpet, made a temporary wire mesh gate and put this in place of the living room door. We then covered the floor with a thick layer of straw and carried Didi down. With the help of another bale of straw, we managed to build a retaining wall behind which Didi was propped so that even when sitting down she was unable to fall on her side. This meant Didi was safe and warm, but we had a few sleepless nights ahead.

Have you ever tried to carry a pile of straw? I defy anyone to move a great armful of straw more than five yards without leaving a trail behind him. Within a couple of hours, the cottage looked like an extension of my neighbour's stack yard or the church just after Harvest Festival, with bits of straw everywhere. The cats and dogs didn't help. They all wanted to get a closer look at this new addition in the passageway and it didn't take them long to invent half a dozen great games which involved dragging lumps of straw round the house or hiding them under the cushions and Suzi even went so far as to bury a lump under my pillow. Suzi is a tiny crossbreed. She looks just like a pot Alsatian, the sort that my Gran used to have on the sideboard. We took turns to spend half the night on the settee, half sleeping and half watching over Didi.

She was just improving and we felt that the time would soon come when we could bring the cottage back to normal – well, our definition of normal, anyway – when the weather took a turn for the worse. It would have been very foolish to risk the effects of such a severe change in temperature on the still very weak goat. At best Didi was never hardy; being an African pygmy goat she detested bad weather, particularly the rain. So we spent almost a month treading straw through the house and hurdling the wire gate every time we needed to go to the loo. It was worth it, as Didi recovered fully, but many months later we were still finding bits of straw in all the secret places that the animals share between them.

All the early breeding birds are well into egg sitting by March and quite a few have already got young in the nest. I say nest, figuratively speaking, as most parrots and parakeets do not actually build a nest. In the wild they usually find suitable cavities in tree trunks and then hollow them out to a suitable depth to keep their precious offspring safe.

It's possible to buy ready-made boxes for most sizes of

bird. However, some birds have different ideas when it comes to the ideal nursery. The most exquisite nest boxes can be decimated in no time at all by a fussy hen. You've also got to bear in mind, when the birds nest in trees, that there's always an automatic source of humidity with the sap rising up through the tree. When eggs fail to hatch, lack of humidity is often one of the main causes. Different breeders have different methods and I would never be one to say that someone else's ideas were wrong. If it works for you, then that's fine. What works for me, I've found, after several frustrating seasons of trial and error, is a mixture of peat and forest bark, both products being regularly available from a garden centre. I always try to mimic wild conditions for my birds, so I generally have to do a bit of decorating before they'll accept my choice of receptacle.

I usually take an ordinary nest box of suitable size, bearing in mind that it doesn't have to accommodate just Mum and Dad, but, if I'm really lucky, several offspring, for quite a few weeks. I start by putting a few inches of peat into the bottom of the box and then a good thick layer of forest bark. This resembles a bed of wood shavings which the birds would have prepared had they been living in the wild.

I know it's a mistake to give animals the same attributes as man, but I do tend to think myself into the place of the creature I'm providing for. If I was a hen parrot, I'd get pretty fed up sitting for a few weeks inside a box with four bare walls. To make life a bit more interesting, I go to the local wood yard and buy a sackful of pine log off-cuts. These are the pieces of wood that are left with the bark on, after the logging yard has put a pine trunk through one of its machines to make square fencing posts. I attach bits of this to the inside of the nest box and these usually last for one season. It not only gives the hen something to do and stops her from destroying the nest box, but also it's quite often used as a ladder by the young when they make their first attempt to look at the outside world.

When breeding any birds I avoid hand rearing wherever possible. Apart from the fact that I believe the natural parents can do an infinitely better job than humans can, however well meaning, it is a hell of a lot of hard work and I have

always been one for avoiding hard work if I can. One year
I had a hen Alexandrine parakeet who had three babies and
while they were very tiny was doing a grand job of rearing
them and being a very good mum. Both parents were very
solicitous towards their offspring, but as soon as they started
to develop feathers, for some reason the mother took an
instant dislike to them. Every time a little feather popped
through she would pull it out. That happens sometimes for
a brief period and then stops, but this particular year this
hen wouldn't stop. Of course the chicks can only take this
treatment for so long, because the formation of feathers takes
an awful lot from their diet. They need a tremendous amount
of calcium and protein and vitamins and minerals and there
is only so much that you can shovel in one end to sustain a
bird if you are pulling out its feathers at the other end.

Finally we decided to remove the chicks and finish off the
rearing process by hand. Otherwise we would certainly have
lost the babies. The problem about hand rearing any birds
that have spent the earliest part of their lives with their
natural parents is getting them used to being fed by humans.
If you start to hand rear birds before their eyes are open
there is no problem at all. They will happily open their beaks
and accept the spoon or syringe or whatever you are using
to feed them. It only takes them a couple of feeds to get
used to the idea that this is where the grub comes from
and in no time at all you will have demented little loonies
frantically begging for you to give them something.

When they have been with their parents for some time
and they know that they are birds and that food comes from
mother's beak, they are not awfully happy about the idea of
this great pair of hands and the spoon attempting to feed
them. We had three reasonably large birds who should have
been well on the way to being fully feathered, not near the
state of independence where they could feed themselves but
needing a lot of extra food and a lot of extra attention and
fighting all the time.

When I am feeding baby birds I wrap them up in a towel,
using it like a shawl, so that just their head is poking out. I
hold the bird and the towel between my knees, which leaves
both hands free to manipulate the implement in their beak.

The problem with parrots, of course, is that the beak is the dodgy end. That is where you get all the problems: if they decide to bite you really know it and even though these birds were quite young, their beaks were well formed. The Alexandrine parakeet has a very large beak and could certainly make a mess of my fingers if it chose to. The one advantage I have over many people is that I have very long and very, very strong finger nails. With a bit of manipulation I can usually wedge a nail in one side of a beak and even though a chick may be trying like mad to bite me it keeps coming up against what appears to be another beak – a couple of my finger nails. These birds fought with everything in their power to stop me from feeding them. I was always covered in this sloppy mass of food, getting very little down into the parrot. When you are hand feeding birds you really should avoid getting any food debris stuck on the bird, because dried food on the beak can make it grow slightly deformed or it can stop feathers coming through if it is on the skin. You have got to be scrupulously clean, but when you are wrestling with a bird this is virtually impossible. Also parrots' food has to be hot, because under normal feeding conditions the food would be regurgitated by the female directly into the baby's beak. If the food is much colder than parrot body temperature, which is quite hot, not only will the chick refuse it, but it can also be quite dangerous because it can impact in the crop of the bird and become a solid mass: then you have got real difficulties trying to clear that mass *and* get the bird to accept more food.

I used a combination of a spoon with the sides bent up over to imitate a parrot's beak and a bowl of hot water with a bowl of the food standing in it so that it kept hot. Picture a parrot with a shawl on, and me trying to balance it between my knees without squashing it and feed it. All this at three or four hourly intervals. If you start rearing birds from the egg it is at much more frequent intervals. Although these birds did not need to be fed quite so often, it still meant feeding them in the middle of the night. When I was waking up at three o'clock in the morning to feed the parrots that was well and truly the middle of the night as far as I was concerned. Not as it is now, my normal waking time. I had a Mothercare baby bottle-warmer next to the bed with the food in. The food consisted of human baby food, various tins of the unsweetened fruit and the beef and vegetable broth mixed together, which gives quite a fair resemblance of the sort of food that the parents would regurgitate for their young. Not a very pleasant prospect at three o'clock in the morning, being covered in mashed fruit and beef broth while trying to get two or three spoonfuls of it into three separate birds. The process usually took at least half an hour and in the morning I would wake up to find that there were crusty bits of beef broth all over me and all over the sheets. Then I would have to begin the whole process again. It really was a struggle and the birds never did succumb properly to the fact that this lunatic human was trying to help them. They fought me every step of the way. They did eventually feather up and were able to be put out into an aviary. There they could watch the birds in the next aviary feeding and they learned very quickly. They are great copycats and in no time at all they were taking their own soft food and sprouted seeds and eventually they moved on to hard seeds. We had reared them successfully. It is not an easy task and not one to be taken on lightly. It is worth it in the end, but it is not an economical process. If you thought for a minute going into parrot production would make you a millionaire, I'm afraid that you would be sorely mistaken. On the face of it the idea sounds quite good: one pair of birds breeding every year, especially the more costly ones. Macaws can fetch several hundred pounds each and if you are prepared to remove the first clutch of eggs and rear the young, then leave the second clutch to the parents, you could have a couple of thousand pounds worth of birds each year. They are long-lived birds – fifty years is not uncommon. Quite a potential income. But what if things go wrong, what if they don't like each other? They won't just mate with any old member of the opposite sex. Most important of all for me is what happens to them. If you breed dozens and just sell them to anyone, who knows what a horrid fate could be in store. I try wherever possible to follow my youngsters, preferably exchanging them for new blood with another breeder.

April

Sunshine and showers, but not always in that order. Blossoms are beginning to be evident on the good old hawthorn, beloved of farmers for fencing in stock. At least the more sensible ones. Who could prefer a barbed wire fence to the tangle of thorns and nutty-tasting leaves? When the hawthorn is covered in white flowers it's a definite sign that spring has sprung. The more flowers, the more berries – good free parrot food of which I take full advantage.

Here's a bit of intellectual stuff – did you know that April comes from the Latin 'aperire', a word describing the opening of a leaf? Nest-building is on with a vengeance and with the new greenery comes an old problem, hay fever. So many people suffer from this allergy, and the hay fever warning will start coming through with the daily weather forecast at the first sign of the warmer weather.

The allergy is one of the most common problems that seems to have taken over in this so-called civilised day and age. Years ago, allergies were virtually unheard of. Perhaps they existed but were never defined as such. Nowadays, allergies to everything are commonly reported in newspapers, magazines and medical journals. I personally suffer from an allergy to most metals, which is why you will never see me wearing jewellery. Not for me the luxury of being showered in diamonds unless they were fitted into the sort of plastic rings you get from Christmas crackers. As I have never been particularly fond of that kind of adornment I can live without it quite happily, but the worst possible thing that could happen to me would be to join that ever-increasing group of people who are allergic to animals. The horse allergy is one of the strongest recorded and its unfortunate sufferers can be badly affected just by standing next to someone who has been near a horse. Cat and dog allergy is quite common and, in a similar vein, not so much an allergy, more a phobia of birds, snakes and spiders is well documented.

One of the most unusual cases I have come across was when I was recording a television piece at London Zoo. On this occasion I was featuring the largest and the smallest members of its vast collection. After a delightful morning with the elephants I was to spend the afternoon at the insect house. This section of the zoo spends a great deal of its time breeding various insects to feed to other animals, birds and reptiles. There was a very enthusiastic young man in charge and after looking round the public area of the insect house, we set up our recording equipment in the private behind-the-scenes breeding area. Half-way through the interview, we had planned that I would handle one of the large red-kneed tarantulas. Tarantula lovers, of which there are many believe it or not, will tell you that it is much safer to handle a female than a male. Females are in general much steadier and not half as unpredictable as the male of the species. Why did I just think of the comparison to humans? This particular female was extremely gentle and despite the fact that she had the ability to give me an extremely nasty bite, which is not fatal but certainly extremely painful, she showed no inclination to do so. In the wild, a tarantula has a very effective form of self-defence. The uninitiated would refer to them as the big hairy spiders and in fact they are thickly covered in fine hairs resembling the very fine spines of a certain kind of cactus plant. If the tarantula is threatened by a predator, its first line of defence is to use its back legs which it rapidly brushes across its abdomen, releasing a cloud of these tiny hairs into the face of its would-be attacker. If you have ever used a roll of fibreglass insulation in your loft without adequate protection, you'll know exactly how it feels.

In the reptile house, the temperature is always kept very high. This speeds up the breeding processes but also makes the human occupants sweat copiously or should I say perspire. What's the old phrase, 'Gentlemen perspire, ladies merely glow'? While I was glowing the reptile keeper was doing his fair share of perspiring. This opens all the pores on the surface of your skin. After the tarantula had left my hand and been passed over to her keeper, she had obviously been irritated by something and furiously rubbed her legs and released her defence mechanism. In the space of thirty seconds, my poor interviewee was choking. He put the spider down and rubbed his watering eyes and scratched his by now red hand and arm. Until this moment I was not aware of the tarantula's special ability and was concerned that my companion had taken an understandable fit of camera nerves. This would have explained his dry throat and coughing and I have often seen people unused to being on television break out in a nervous red blotchy rash, but this is usually found around the chest and neck line. (Look out for it next time you see someone on television with a low neckline. Make-up artists, however good, can't hide something that appears in mid-performance.) The poor keeper was eventually able to explain to us that he suffered a severe allergy to tarantula hair. I asked him later when he was slightly recovered why on earth he did the job; he explained that apart from the fact that he loved the insects it was a great line when asked about his job to pull girls at parties.

When you work in television, it's just like any other job – you become familiar with the techniques and pretty blasé about the whole thing. I must admit, the only thing that still really holds magic for me is the cinema. I've worked in radio, I've worked in television and I know many of the tricks of the trade. But the big screen is still quite a mystery to me and I do enjoy regular visits. What I don't like about any part of the media is when they use animals out of context and give them a bad reputation.

One good thing that television in particular does, is to bring the magic of the natural world into our living rooms. Over the years, I've watched thousands of animal programmes, never dreaming, until recently, that I would be in the privileged position that I am today, able to speak to millions of people in one go. I'm very lucky to have the chance to inform, educate and amuse, and I try to put the case for caring for all our animal friends over to as many people as possible. I remember when I was quite young reading books by Konrad Lorenz. This man has truly remark-able powers of observation and an uncanny ability to communicate with the animals around him. Quite often I couldn't understand all of his books the first time around, but they whetted my appetite so that I made sure it wasn't long before I did. I remember seeing a marvellous documen-tary on this man – one of my all time heroes. He was already quite old and not up to the antics that he was able to perform in his youth. But have you noticed that people with a genuine enthusiasm and love of their chosen subject never really seem to grow old? They're always busy, always discovering something new, and seem to find the greatest joy of all in sharing their passion with others. Quite a number of people that I've met over the years in the animal world are like this. It often gives me visions of the future with me as an eighty-year-old nutcase in green wellies and an old mac, still plodding round my garden talking to birds that I've bred recently, who if they live their natural age span will certainly outlive me.

The image that sticks in my mind most from the Konrad Lorenz documentary, is of a wonderful man with a weathered face, a mass of white hair and beard, a lovely accent, but most of all, bright twinkling eyes. They say the eyes are the window to the soul – I'm sure there's a lot of truth in it. Think of the happiest person you know and I bet their happiness is reflected in their eyes. Mr Lorenz – I hold him too much in awe to presume to use his first name – lives in a beautiful house surrounded by the most magnificent countryside. As he is not quite as fit as he perhaps would like, he's brought his work indoors to continue his studies in a more comfortable setting. His work on imprinting, particularly with greylag geese and the behaviour of jackdaws, is renowned. But now he has turned his skill and still very active mind to the study of the coral reef. Obviously he's not at liberty to don a wetsuit and snorkel and pop out to the Great Barrier Reef, so 'when Mohammed can't go to the mountain', at least a bit of the Barrier Reef comes to the living room. One wall of his study appeared to be made entirely of glass and behind it was the most magnificent aquarium I'd ever seen. With thousands of gallons of seawater being filtered and aerated every day, Mr Lorenz was able to sit and observe the interaction between a whole colony of fish, coral and all the other marvellous things that are familiar to those of us who have been glued to our television sets since the early days and have explored with Jacques Cousteau.

The nearest thing to this that I've ever had was a tank containing Oswald.

A few years ago I was in a pet shop, as usual. If you ask people directions, it's a dead giveaway as to where their interests lie. My auntie would tell you how to get somewhere via the churches that are en route, lots of my friends could tell you all the pubs en route. I don't think many people would direct you via the pet shops, but that's the way I find myself moving around a strange town. I find the pet shops that I have seen advertised in various trade magazines and go and have a look.

Anyway, I was in this pet shop. At the time I was quite keen on tropical fish; I had quite a few fish tanks on the go and I was looking for something a little bit different, though nothing too expensive because as usual I was poor and was spending every penny I had on the animals. The owner of this shop was obviously a keen aquarist. It's always nice to see this when you go into a pet shop – you can tell, as soon as you walk through the door, whether the people are in it purely for the money or because it is a hobby that developed into a job. If these people manage to make a living that's fine, but the most important thing for them is to be in contact with animals. You usually find lots of people in that sort of shop because they are all enthusiasts as well and they are encouraged to go in and talk together. This shop was obviously an aquarists' mecca. They were all there studying the form outside the tanks, just as keen as punters studying the line-up at the Grand National, commenting on posture and fin and colour and the general sort of chit-chat that can seem so foreign to someone who isn't involved in the hobby. They were all hard at it when I went in and I joined in a little bit, cos I can't keep my mouth shut for long, and while I was talking I saw a tank out of the corner of my eye. It had about half a dozen small fish in it which I didn't recognise. Well, the only way to improve your knowledge is to ask, and I was told that they were juvenile osphronemus goramies. Experts tend to show off with the Latin names. As it happens I'd acquired several different members of the gorami family recently, and was hoping to breed them, so I was keen to learn as much about them as I could. Fish seem to be imported in batches: obviously it is something to do with the country of origin and every so often you will get a flush of a certain kind of fish going around the shops. The goramies were very attractive fish and in the main they had proved to be easy going. Sometimes you put a fish into a tank with a lot of others and go down the next day and find one big fat fish in the corner who has spent his whole night devouring the rest of his tank mates. But goramies seem very peace loving. They are particularly interesting because they are labyrinths, which means that they breathe some air in the same way as we do, as well as having gills. They come up to the surface and gulp air and when they lay eggs they blow bubbles which make a nest: the bubbles are slightly adhesive, and they stick together.

I had not heard of these particular goramies before, so I thought the best thing to do was to buy one and take it home. Then I would find out more about it and what its requirements were, and buy a few more if it worked. Of course, if I was sticking to the proper animal owner's guidelines I wouldn't be buying it at all at this point. I would be going home and finding out what it was and then coming back. However, I was given a piece of advice years and years ago that I have proceeded to ignore ever since: never buuy an animal on impulse. I'm afraid that my whole life is lived on impulses, so I'm not going to stop where the biggest love of my life is concerned.

I took this osphronemus goramy home and christened him Oswald. I put him into a quarantine tank. Good aquarists always keep newly bought fish in a separate tank for a couple of weeks to make sure they don't develop any contagious illnesses. It is dreadful to lose a tank full of healthy fish just because you can't be bothered with simple hygiene precautions. I'd been told by the pet shop owner that he had had these fish for about three months, so it was very unlikely that they had a disease, but I still popped it into the quarantine tank just in case. Everything went well and Oswald didn't bully anybody. He was quite a small chap really and thoroughly insignificant looking, mid-brownish with a few stripes and nothing outstanding to look at.

When I eventually found a book that described these fish in detail, I must admit that I was rather taken aback. Little Oswald, this little inoffensive brown speck in the tank, had every chance of growing up to two feet long in the wild. The species originates in the Great Sunda Islands, part of Indonesia, and is caught and eaten as a food fish.

There is one thing that I always remember when buying living creatures: if I buy something then I take it on for life. An animal in my care only moves on to another owner if that other owner is looking for a mate for theirs or if we have done a swop to exchange blood lines or if it is going to the right home, somebody who really cares. I'm not just going to fob something off on somebody else just because I'm sick of it or because I've made a mistake or I've got the loony in the bunch. So Oswald was here to stay. And he grew and grew and grew.

His rate of growth was quite phenomenal. He soon had to be moved out of the tank with the other smaller fish in because now he was much bigger than any other fish I owned and even though he was such a sweetheart and lovely natured he couldn't help but notice these little tasty morsels that were swimming by. At this time I was living in a flat over a general dealer and newsagent-type shop, in the north east of England. I was looking for somewhere else to live, partly because my landlord was a bit unreasonable, but mostly because I wanted somewhere with a garden so that I could expand the animal collection a bit more. In the meantime I was keeping the only things that it was really practical to keep inside a flat and that included fish tanks. As Oswald grew, he outgrew the accommodation I had available and I rapidly realised that I would have to get something much bigger if he was going to continue to grow at the rate he should have grown in the wild. Lots of creatures can have their growth retarded by inadequate living space, particularly reptiles and fish. They grow to suit the space available, so if you don't expand their accommodation with their expanding girth you will find stunted, very unhappy and unhealthy creatures that usually become incapable of breeding and never reach their full potential in life.

Oswald was provided with a six foot by two foot by one and a half foot tank which had been specially made out of quarter-inch plate glass and was on its own purpose built, angle iron metal stand. He had pride of place in the living room. Oswald was the only fish that I have ever known who lived within the room rather than within the tank. You can keep tanks and tanks of tropical fish around and although the fish will swim to the top in readiness as soon as you approach the tank at the usual time of day to feed them, as a general rule they are not aware of activity going on around the room. Oswald was incredible. It was like having my own little dolphinarium right in the middle of my living room. I spent whole nights watching Oswald and totally ignored the television. He was such a character. I didn't have any sort of lid on the tank because he was such a messy feeder – normally with a fish tank you'd have a complete ecosystem in the tank, with a little filter constantly cleaning the water and recycling the waste to feed the plants, but with Oswald it was easier to have no lid on and just keep sticking a very powerful Eheim filter in the water after he had fed to clean out any impurities.

Oswald rapidly realised that there was food to be had if he was a bit crafty and in the summer when we had lots and lots of flies in the flat it was as good as going to Disneyland, just to sit in my living room and watch Oswald. He would swim up and down in his leisurely manner – of course by this time he was so big that with a couple of flicks of his tail he went from one end of the tank to the other, and head on he was several inches across. He was a massive fish and a couple of flicks of his tail used fairly to churn the water up. He would swim up and down quite contentedly and then a fly would start buzzing round the top of the tank. He would stop and sort of roll half sideways to get one eye to look up and spot this fly. Of course, his eyes were situated on either side of his head and he had to look with one or the other.

I have always been astounded by the accuracy and skill with which archer fish catch their prey. They swim just below the surface of the water and look up. If they see a fly or a cricket or something dangling on a piece of greenery just above the surface, they squirt a jet of water and knock the prey off the leaf. It falls down on to the surface of the water and they grab it and eat it. I have always wondered how they manage to compensate for the lack of eye line, looking upwards out of the water. You know that if you open your eyes under water, your sense of distance is completely distorted. But the archer fish is deadly accurate and Oswald must have had one or two archer fish somewhere among his ancestors because he was just amazing. He didn't have the facility to squirt water. What he did have was an extremely strong tail that would allow him to flip his whole body weight out of the water and do an impression of Flipper the dolphin. The flies would be buzzing around, quite unaware of what was awaiting them. Oswald would eye them up, roll over slightly to one side like a sick submarine, peering up through the water. His one visible eye would roll and then all of a sudden he would shoot out of the water and grab a fly. He wasn't quite the Robin Hood of the fish world. He did a lot of belly-flops before he caught anything to put in his belly, but he managed in the end. He also succeeded in drenching everything anywhere near his tank. The wall behind the tank used to get soaked.

Oswald continued to grow and continued to live in the room and not in the tank. He could go through a heck of a lot of food. I used to go down to the garden behind the shop and dig up worms to feed him and bring them upstairs in a jam jar. One evening Oswald must have been particularly hungry. I had been out collecting a load of worms. By the time I came upstairs, the shop downstairs was closed, thank God, because what happened in the next half hour would probably have got me evicted. When I came in carrying the jam jar Oswald was at one end of his tank and he spotted me. He used to get excited if I came into the room even with a coffee cup in my hand because he obviously thought it was his jam jar full of worms.

On this occasion he was right. He flicked his tail to speed down the tank towards me and didn't stop. By this time he weighed several pounds; his full weight crashed against the end of the tank and I am afraid that he kept on going. The end of the tank cracked, burst open under the pressure of over a hundred gallons of water, and within a minute Oswald was flapping around on the floor in a mixture of broken glass, carpet and water. The hundred gallons of water had spilled out into the flat.

As always my first concern was the animal. The only time that I have ever had a car accident, I hit a dog. I was moving very slowly and the dog dashed out of a side road: in fact the dog hit me, rather than the other way round, but I was absolutely devastated. My car could have been a write-off and I wouldn't even have noticed. I just jumped out, leaving the car in the middle of the road, and ran off down the back streets to follow this dog to make sure it was okay.

So with Oswald slopping around in broken glass on the floor all I was worried about was getting him up and out of it. I ran into the kitchen and pulled the plastic bag bin-liner out of the bin with all the rubbish in it. I grabbed the bottom half of the big plastic bin and just poured a lot of water in it as quickly as possible. At this point I didn't worry about the condition of the water, it was more critical to get him out of the mess on the carpet and the broken glass than bother about giving him a shock with the wrong type of water – I thought he had already suffered enough shock not to fuss about anything more. I filled up the bin and then thought, 'God, how am I going to pick him up?' I grabbed a towel out of the bathroom, wet it and wrapped it round him. At this point I realised how big and enormously heavy he was.

He was very, very frightened and he was twitching and flicking his tail like mad. One flick of his tail caught me badly and my forefinger went totally out of joint. So I was screaming in agony, but I got the fish into the bin and he seemed quite okay. He was so tough – he didn't even had a cut. I had a dislocated finger on one hand. Three fingers lacerated with broken glass on the other. I had ruined a pair of shoes. The flat looked as if it was suffering from the after effects of Niagara Falls being diverted via my living room. The carpets were squelchy and there were streams running along the skirting boards, but the bulk of the water – and there was a hell of a lot of it – had gone.

The last thing that occurred to me was what had happened to it. I was so worried about Oswald and what I was going to do with him that I couldn't think of anything else. I rang a friend in the Aquarist Society who had a supply of large fibreglass tubs. They were formerly ammunition carriers, apparently, but they were very useful for keeping all kinds of things in. This friend was just as fanatical about the whole business as I was, so he came straight round with a tub that was a more sensible shape for Oswald to live in. While the rubbish bin had probably saved his life, it was still very uncomfortable because he was having to swim standing on his tail. I filled up the ammunition carrier and I transferred Oswald without any problem. We took up the carpet and fortunately it dried out reasonably well. It was the standard thing you get when you rent a furnished flat: it had been good once but was now very old. When the landlord has something he doesn't want to use in his own house he slings it into the rented property. The carpet wasn't fitted to start with and it did shrink a bit, but I wasn't unduly worried about that: it looked a lot brighter after the thorough washing and came out better than pre-flood.

The funny part was the next morning when the landlord knocked on the flat door at something like 4.30 a.m. (he started early to sort out the newspapers) and said, 'Have you left a tap on in the bathroom?' I snapped, 'No.' I was very annoyed at being awoken at that hour. He said, 'Well, I don't know what has happened. I've got two boxes of toilet rolls downstairs that are soaking wet and they've expanded so much that they have blocked a doorway.' I looked at him straight in the face and said, 'Well, I'm sorry but it's really nothing to do with me and I would appreciate not being woken up at this time in future' and I went back to bed.

Of course, Oswald couldn't live permanently in the ammunition carrier: we had to come to an alternative arrangement. I was willing to get an even larger tank made for him but I was told that the actual structure of the flat wouldn't take any more weight in tank and water. Water is extremely heavy and so I had to think of something else. I remembered when I was a child going to Bellevue Zoo in Manchester. They had huge aquariums there with all sorts of amazing fish and I felt sure that they would have several osphronemus goramies. Oswald had grown into the fish he was meant to be – a big, fat, prime adult. It would have been best to keep him with several of his own kind but that would be absolutely impossible in a normal house, never mind a flat above a shop. So I rang Bellevue and they confirmed that they did have three other Oswalds and yes, they would be quite willing to take mine if I could get him over there.

I had to hire a minibus, put the giant ammunition carrier complete with Oswald in the back and drive up to Bellevue, but I had a wonderful day when I eventually got there. It was my first look behind the scenes in a zoo. It was great. The people in the reptile house and the aquarium really made me feel at home and I got to go in the enclosures with the giant tortoises and the adult iguanas and all these things just add more bricks to my wall of enthusiasm. It's like a giant Lego: every time I have a new animal experience I add it to the pile and it just gets bigger and bigger and takes over more and more of my life. It was wonderful to see Oswald in an enormous tank that I could never have given him, swimming around quite happily with others of his own kind. Many years later Bellevue Zoo closed down and I rang up to find out what was happening to the fish. They said that they were going off to another large aquarium somewhere else. I just hope that they weren't fobbing me off. I would like to think that Oswald was still floating around, eyeing flies somewhere.

The whole structure of this planet is based on one thing living off another. Even vegetarians are predators living on plant life which is grown by nature's process of recycling. Oswald, much loved by me as a pet, would have been a sought-after table delicacy had he stayed in his native surroundings. In fact fish as a food support millions of other creatures.

One of the most beautiful fish-eating birds can be seen in this country. I've been guilty, and I'm sure you have too, of marvelling at the beauty of a bird of paradise or a tiny jewelled humming bird and thinking, however briefly, that it's always exotic countries that are the homes of the most magnificent members of the bird family. Rarer though the sight may be, it's still possible to wander on the banks of Britain's waterways and discover one of the most beautiful birds of all. I had a very close encounter and was fortunate enough to make the intimate acquaintance of a young kingfisher.

Over the years there has certainly been a predominance of birds in the Willis's animal collection. We've had a great variety in our care, everything from the humble sparrow to the magnificent heron and all sorts of shapes and sizes in between. A lot of individual characters stand out in my mind. Birds are difficult to treat in many cases because a wild bird does not often come into our care until it is beyond saving. It struggles on and by the time it is actually weak enough to pick up, it is usually too late for us to do anything for it. We always try, though, and despite a lot of failures the successes make it all worthwhile.

Enter the kingfisher. Its colours are so extraordinary, that beautiful iridescent turquoise and the autumn-coloured breast with the orangy-gold and brown feathers. It is such a perfect little bird, designed exactly for its niche in the ecological ladder. It eats our smaller fish, and has an extremely large beak in proportion to the rest of its body. Its short wings are designed for quick bursts of flight both above and below the surface of the water. It is vulnerable in bad winters when the open waters are frozen for long periods – like all specialised feeders, it cannot make do with anything other than its regular diet.

This particular kingfisher came to me after a bank on our local river had collapsed because of heavy rain one April. There had been some removal of trees the winter before and as the roots were dying off in the ground, the land was much more likely to subside. People tend to forget this. They cut down a tree, ignoring the fact that the life and the roots of the tree are holding the area together; and once they start to die off the whole area is in danger. This is exactly what happened to the kingfisher's nest which was in the edge of the bank.

Kingfishers excavate a tunnel in the bankside. The entrance is well above the water line to avoid flooding. A cosy if somewhat smelly chamber will be found at the end of the tunnel: if your diet was exclusively raw fish and you could never get out of the house I feel your home would smell a bit. Telltale white deposits can often be spotted on the bankside and the parents will not be far away, perched on their regular feeding places.

51

This kingfisher's nest was completely exposed but fortunately most of the babies appeared to have just left the nest, and only one kingfisher remained. Quite often one of a clutch of young birds is smaller and weaker than the rest – the chick which hatches last is constantly domineered by the rest of the siblings and gets food only when everyone else is full. A vicious circle develops. The chick doesn't grow as fast as the others and never really catches up. This kingfisher chick was presumably left behind in the nest when the parents abandoned it after the riverbank had been destroyed, and it was brought to me. Luckily it was virtually fully fledged and so didn't need a great deal of attention as far as heat was concerned, but I did make a substitute kingfisher nest so that it would feel more secure in the dark. Once it was in its little artificial kingdom I attempted to feed it.

As I said earlier, it is a relatively easy task to make a baby bird take food from your hand if it hasn't got totally imprinted on its parents. But this kingfisher was about to go out into the world and learn about feeding for itself. For the first three or four hours I found myself covered in bits of fish as it wrestled with me. I managed to keep its bill firmly clamped tight while I was shredding bits of whitebait in all directions and generally stinking like an old fishwife down on the quayside. It is funny and frustrating when you are trying your very best to help this creature survive and it seems to be doing its damnedest to thwart your good intentions. Eventually with a combination of patience, skill and plain brute force, I managed to get it to swallow some fish but I realised that this wasn't going to be very satisfactory. I decided to wean it extremely early and teach it how to catch fish for itself.

Local children and their mercenary tendencies are always excellent allies when I am seeking certain kinds of wild food. I have often paid children 50p for a large bag of rosehips when I have been sick of ripping my fingers to shreds picking them around the hedgerows. They are wonderful food for parrots. I have also paid 20p a jam jar for worms at ploughing time when the children follow the plough and rob the seagulls of their bounty so that I have a ready supply of worms for whatever happens to be needing that particular food.

This time I called upon my local network of helpers to provide me with minnows from the local stream and with a price on the head of every minnow I soon had sufficient to ensure the survival of the kingfisher – if only I could teach it that it was supposed to eat them and not cover me in them.

You might be reading this and wondering how I can talk so glibly about the death of one creature sustaining another. Fish are living creatures too, of course, but that is the way nature works. The minnows were part of a big food chain and as long as there was no cruelty involved then it was up to me to give the kingfisher the best chance I could. The best chance meant teaching it to catch its own food and its own food in nature would be these small fish.

I built a little fibreglass pool in the animal room with branches sticking out on all sides so that the kingfisher could perch on the branches over the water as he would in the wild. Then I put half a dozen minnows in the pond, stood the kingfisher on the branch and hid to see what would happen. All the minnows swam around in the pond blissfully ignorant of their forthcoming fate and the kingfisher stood on the branch, seemingly equally blissfully ignorant about what he was supposed to do with these minnows in the pond below. Reluctantly after two or three hours I decided that he must be fed again because all birds, particularly smaller birds, need to feed very, very often; they are the ones that die rapidly in the winter when food isn't readily available.

A bad winter always decimates the population of blue-tits, wrens and all of the tiny birds because their metabolic rate is such that they need to feed constantly. The cold gets to ill-fed little birds much quicker than it does to ill-fed larger birds. The kingfisher was in very warm surroundings but I still felt I should feed him again. On the previous occasion I had been using whitebait, which are somewhat larger than minnows, and it was rather difficult to get the whole fish into the kingfisher's mouth and make him swallow. This time I had a few minnows and it made life a little simpler. I managed to get a couple of minnows down the kingfisher's throat and then left him to digest them for a while, hoping that he would get the gist of what he was supposed to do. A couple of hours later, when I felt that he must be hungry again, I went into the room and he was still sitting on the same branch. He hadn't moved a feather. I took a couple of freshly killed minnows and put them in the water with the live ones, dragged them around a little bit in the water and then picked them out and popped them into his beak. This time it seemed marginally easier than the last couple of times and I felt that perhaps he was getting the hang of it, or maybe he was not quite as well as I thought and was just giving in.

This can often be the case, with wild birds in particular. You think suddenly that you have made progress and in fact you haven't made any progress at all, it is the bird that is going into decline and isn't struggling any more. Just when you think you have won something round and it is on the road to recovery, that thing goes and dies on you. Over all the years and with all the animals I have ever taken care of, I've never found it easy to accept the death of anything. One thing that I wasn't willing to contemplate was the death of this kingfisher. It was so magnificent and I was going to do everything in my power to make sure it stayed that way.

I spent hours going through a ridiculous performance of tying a dead minnow to a bit of cotton, pulling it through the water and flicking it out of the water to attract the kingfisher's attention, trying to encourage it to eat. Eventually, slowly but surely the penny dropped and after a few days, the kingfisher decided that it had to work a bit on its own behalf. By this time it was taking regular feeds from me without much trouble but I was leaving it alone as often as possible so that it didn't become too familiar with humans. There's always a danger that a creature you've cared for begins to feel that all humans are going to be good to be around. Inevitably there is good and bad everywhere and the human animal appears to have an awful lot of the bad where animals are concerned. The incidents of absolutely blatant, stupid cruelty that I have had to try and put right after some idiot with an air gun has used a beautiful bird for target practice just sicken me to my stomach. I was going to

54

make sure that the kingfisher wasn't going to be some loony's target next week.

Hiding behind the peep hole into the animal room is really where I find out most things. All creatures will sit and be as good as gold when I am there, but there is a small window in the door of the animal room and I have covered all except a tiny corner of that. I spend a lot of time in the corridor watching through this little peep hole to see what is going on when my back is turned. It reminds me of a story that I read and thought was absolutely magical when I was a child, about all the toys coming to life in your bedroom as soon as you go to sleep. I was convinced that all my teddies and cuddly toys had a great time while I was asleep and watching through the peep hole is a sort of extension of that. The kingfisher, thinking I was safely out of the way, would fly down and stand on a little rock that was jutting out of the pool. He would watch the fish for a while, then fly back up to his perch, stab his beak in the water a few times and then groom and preen and generally make himself look magnificent. He would then sit on the perch and wait to be fed. This went on for quite some time and then one day, when I wasn't looking . . . Of course the really good things always seem to happen when you are not there, just that second when you have turned your back something miraculous occurs. In this case the kingfisher obviously went in and caught his first minnow, because when I went into the pond the next time there were only five. On such an occasion you keep counting over and over again because you can't believe your eyes. I had counted so many fish swimming up and down – minnows are fast movers – that eventually, although I was convinced that it was five, I had to get a second opinion, and yes it was five. So I knew the kingfisher had made it.

The following day tragedy was to strike again. I had been out of the house for a couple of hours and when I got home I went straight to check all the animals, as I always do. I found the kingfisher floating in the pond, beak down, wings spread, apparently drowned. Young kingfishers often drown when they are first learning to catch fish and misjudge their dives. I picked him straight out of the water, held him in my hand and burst into tears. Just as I did that I saw a tiny flicker in the kingfisher's eye. I shook him to get any water out of his lungs, then put his beak completely in my mouth and breathed into it. I did this three or four times, just gently breathing into the kingfisher's mouth, mouth to beak resuscitation, and it worked. I didn't think for a minute that I could catch some horrible disease. It doesn't occur to me in times of desperation. I'm afraid that I have probably taken some pretty stupid risks, but at the time all that matters is doing everything you can to save the life that you have fought so hard for. The kingfisher came round. He was very bedraggled and I immediately put him into a hospital cage at 90°F to recuperate, which he did very rapidly. Birds go down hill very quickly, but they also come back very quickly. Again this is to do with their very high metabolic rate and in no time at all the kingfisher was back in perfect condition. Over the next couple of weeks he managed to catch the rest of the minnows in the pond, and quite a few more that had been added, and I felt confident enough to release him back into the wild. It's a great moment, but also a sad one, because you inevitably come to care very much for whatever is in your charge. However at the end of the day you are doing what you are doing to enable an animal to live its normal life and so off the kingfisher went to an area not far from where he had been born. I released him in the middle of one morning to give him a chance to get his bearings before dark. I made sure he had lots of food inside of him and then just opened the box and watch him fly away. Thereafter all you can do is keep your fingers crossed.

That stretch of water runs through my neighbours' farm, and they say that they still see kingfishers down there. I like to think that one of them is the one that I released and that he lived to mate and breed and continue the line of those magnificent little birds.

May

Warmer weather takes its time to travel north and it is really only in May that the earth is alive with growing things. Nearly everywhere lovely fresh shades of green make an exciting change in the landscape. Only the ash tree still persists in keeping its bleak winter face. Next month it will get its new clothes, but for now the miserable ~od will make do.

Many people who live in the south of England have a very misguided feeling about the north. Despite many promotion campaigns and such marvellous books as the James Herriot series, the image of the cloth cap and the miner still prevails. It would be nice if we could all have an opportunity of living in different parts of the country some time in our lives. Having worked on the *Treasure Hunt* series opened my eyes to the diversity of landscape and the beauty of the buildings from one end of the British Isles to the other. Where I live near the Durham/Yorkshire border is still one of my favourite places. It only takes me an hour to drive to the coast and to walk along miles of deserted beach, clamber through sand dunes and experience the glory of the North Sea. To get there I must travel through a highly industrialised area but that too has its own kind of beauty. Much of our native wildlife has taken advantage of the odd pieces of wasteland situated between the giant chemical plants famous in the north east. Breeding colonies of some of our rarer birds have been established in scaffolding after the disappearance of much of their natural habitat. One of Britain's very few kittiwake breeding groups is to be found each year on a large red brick flour mill on the quayside in the heart of Newcastle. Thousands of migrating wild fowl depend on the brackish marshy areas around the estuaries of the north east's larger rivers to stop over and replenish their food store on their journey north or south. Inland and not far from my cottage, there are hundreds of acres of desolate moorland, again with a beauty all their own. Rich men pay up to a thousand pounds a day to come and shoot the moorland grouse. Probably like me you find the whole practice pretty distasteful, but without their money which funds the management of the moors, the whole character of the area would change and most of the wildlife would disappear. Many plants and animals now depend on tiny pockets of land left to its own devices to supply the food and shelter that they need. Few people can fail to notice the abundance of one of our most successful birds of prey, the kestrel, on its hunting trips along the motorway verges. Most of these grassy banks are left untouched by human predators or by cultivation. Many of our native wild plants have virtually disappeared from their original sites but seeds blown on the wind have taken possession of these tiny areas of undisturbed sanctuary. Roadside verges around my cottage still show signs of how the landscape used to be when most of the area was covered in woodland. Since deforestation most of the broad-leaved trees have disappeared but at ground level there are still signs of the forest floor plant life: tiny pockets of bluebells still survive and one of my favourite flowers, the primrose, can still be seen tenaciously holding on to life. Each year it makes me feel good when I first see those tiny yellow heads poking through the grass seeking the still weak northern sunshine.

A few years ago, while I was walking the dogs not far from the cottage, I spotted a council employee driving a small tractor along one of the distant verges, heading in the direction of the cottage. When I got close I asked him what he was doing and he said he had been sent out to spray the verges. 'With what?' I asked but he didn't know. He was a typical jobsworth – you know the sort, 'It's more than my job's worth to ask questions, I've just got to go out and do it.' I then asked him what he was spraying against. He said his boss had muttered something about all the dandelion seedheads clogging up the drains and he had to get rid of them. This meant one thing, weedkiller. Some people consider all wild flowers as weeds and certainly to my know-ledge there was no specific poison designed to eradicate only the dandelions. Apart from my more obvious concern for some of the rarer plants in the tractor's path, I did not particularly want to see all the dandelions killed off either. Each year I use hundreds of dandelion plants to supplement the food of many of my animals. They are an excellent source of nutrition, tortoises love them and parrots, particularly when they are feeding their young, consume copious quantities of both the flower and the leaves. If my captive animals eat them, then surely the local wildlife will be doing the same, so the council would be poisoning not only the plants but potentially many of the animals too. I understand that for purely economical reasons farmers must eradicate weeds growing in their fields as these native plants compete very successfully with the foreign, hybridised versions of the crops grown today. All the more reason, therefore, to leave the verges as undisturbed as possible.

I dashed home and tried to telephone the local council but as usual it was impossible to speak to anyone with any kind of authority. As the minutes ticked by, the tractor was coming nearer. Only two hundred yards from the cottage on the other side from the tractor was one of my precious pockets of primroses and across the road and another hundred yards down was another small group. It is against the law to uproot wild flowers, which I agree with wholeheartedly, but what was the point of obeying the law if leaving them in the ground meant that they would certainly die? I plead guilty, your Honour. I had already told the tractor driver in no uncertain terms that he could not spray along the verge that bordered my garden, which I kept cut down and tidy anyway, and he had decided to cross the road to recommence his deadly work on the opposite verge. I had little time to waste, so armed with a bucket and shovel I ran down to the primroses and carefully removed them in one intact clump. With those safely back at the cottage I then tried to ring the council again – this time it was worse than ringing Directory Enquiries. I got absolutely nowhere – the grapevine had obviously worked and the word was out about this nutcase woman who was ringing up complaining about those bloody primroses.

No-one was available to speak to me at all. I am sure even the tea-lady would have refused my call. By this time the tractor had disappeared into the distance along the far side of the road. It's most peculiar how when you want the council to do something it takes them for ever and when you don't they work at the speed of light. Statutory lunch time was approaching so I knew that the diligent driver would probably have stopped off at the next village for his break. I checked up with my neighbour to try and find out if he knew more than I did about the latest council policies. He was totally unaware of it and was also equally upset: despite the fact that he is a farmer and regularly sprays his fields, he was not happy at all at the idea of the council spraying willy nilly right next to his crops with some unknown poison on a fairly windy day. Even on a light breeze, those fine mist sprays can drift quite some distance and a short while later this was proven as the edge of Douglas's field bordering the verge showed distinct signs of dying oil seed rape plants. He then tried to phone the local authority but of course it was now lunch time – even if he had been trying to pay his rates, no one would have wanted to know until after two o'clock.

As I have mentioned on several occasions, my neighbour's wife's cooking is some of the best I have ever tasted. Pans were bubbling on the Aga and the smell of a lovely roast was escaping from the oven. Marjorie always seems to cater for far more than her family's needs and as it is against my nature to let anything go to waste I was more than happy to accept the invitation to stay and share the goodies. Weekday lunches on the farm are always a bit chaotic with different members of the family arriving at different times in various states of undress. This is usually due to the fact that they have spent the morning doing particularly dirty jobs relating to pig management or even worse artificially inseminating the cows. They have strict instructions to enter by the back passageway and leave smelly wellies and overalls outside the door. They may be immune to the stink but Marjorie isn't and somehow the smell of a slurry pit does nothing to whet one's appetite.

Much later I returned to the cottage feeling very fraught and with a plate laden with Marjorie's homemade fresh cream filled chocolate eclairs for Malcolm because he had missed out on his lunch. As I left the farmhouse I could hear the parrots screeching in the distance, the call that tells me a stranger or something different is approaching their territory. It is marvellous how when you live with animals you learn to speak their language – not in the Doctor Doolittle fashion, but observation over a long period will teach you what each sound means. I can sit indoors and know exactly what is going on out in the back garden well out of my line of sight. Getting nearer to the cottage I realised with horror that just as my lunch had ended so had the tractor driver's. He was now spreading death along the verge on the same side of the road as the cottage and approaching the second batch of primroses.

In law I had no jurisdiction whatsoever over the verges not adjacent to my land. However, I had broken the law once that day so I was not going to let a small matter like that stop me now. But this time I had no chance to collect my bucket and shovel, the tractor was far too close for comfort. The only thing I could possibly do was to mount a one woman protest. Armed with my plate of chocolate eclairs I ran towards the tractor, but he kept on coming. I shouted at him to stop but from under his cap he muttered something about having to get the job done by tea time, so I did the only thing I could in the circumstances and sat down on the grass verge between the tractor and the primroses. At this point I felt extremely lonely – protesting on your own is not much fun. I can understand the camaraderie of the 60's sit-in for peace, as apart from sharing common beliefs there was a sense of achievement at sharing the discomfort and even perhaps the possible prosecution that could follow.

I wondered how much the driver really believed his job was worth, especially as tractors look enormous from ground level. It was then I knew what a vole felt like fleeing from the path of the combine harvester as it relentlessly surges forward. Too close for comfort, the tractor finally ground to a halt, the driver got out of his seat and turned his cap back to front, a sure sign in the country that he meant business. As I have already said, it was a fairly windy day and I was hardly suitably dressed for my current occupation of the verge. It's stupid how your mind works at times like these: clutching my plate of eclairs I mentally reassured myself that even though I may die of exposure I certainly would not starve to death. He told me not to be bloody silly and get out of the way so that he could get on with his work. I tried to explain that I had no intention of moving – if it took all day and all night I was going to save the flowers. To the occasional passing motorist, it must have made a very bizarre spectacle. Muttering obscenities, the dealer of death explained that it wouldn't be all night as he knocked off at four o'clock. That made me feel a bit better as I realised that I only had one and a half hours to go. He sat back on the tractor, made a roll-up cigarette and appeared to be equally determined to sit me out. We all use displacement activity when we are in an uneasy positon. He smoked his cigarette and I ate one of the eclairs. The picture of this bizarre roadside picnic must have left quite a few people puzzled as they drove past the cottage. Two more roll-up cigarettes later and one more eclair (poor Malcolm was rapidly losing his treat) the tractor driver relented. After muttering something about bloody stupid townies, he reversed the tractor and chunked off down the road. Why should he complain, he had got an early finish? I was triumphant, my primroses were safe and by the next day, with the combined efforts of me and my neighbour, we had secured a promise that no further spraying would occur in our vicinity. In the light of what happened to the crops, the council should have thanked me. My neighbour claimed for compensation for his dead produce, a claim which would have been much greater had I not held my sit-in.

My break into television came from a brief appearance on a programme on Tyne Tees Television called *Saturday Shake-Up*. An ex-radio colleague of mine, Alastair Pirrie, was the presenter of the programme. Alastair, I'm sure, has been an eccentric from the day he was born. One of those larger than life, unpredictable human beings whom you encounter rarely. It's strange, but I've always been attracted to eccentrics of any age. They do say birds of a feather flock together, so I suppose that says something about me.

Alastair got up to all sorts of lunacy on the radio and he and I co-presented a Saturday morning programme, before his move into television. He was an extremely talented radio presenter and had that rare ability of being able to turn up with thirty seconds to go before the start of the show and do the slickest three hour programme you could hope to listen to, without one minute's preparation beforehand. It used to drive me barmy, but I was also slightly in awe of his ability to perform in this way. Television, by its nature, has to be more disciplined. Let's face it, you can't present a television programme with your hair standing on end, looking like death and wearing your slippers and get away with it for long, although some say I run close to it. I didn't envy his producer and director, trying to keep him in order. Chaos still reigned on his television programme, but it was never totally out of control. I'm sure because of him people felt that it was instantaneous television, and the programme became extremely popular.

One morning the phone rang and that familiar voice said, 'Now you old tart, how're you doin'?' Alastair is not one to ring you for an idle chat, unless he is completely pissed, not that I'm suggesting he's a drunk. So I said, 'What can I do for you, Alastair?' He said, 'We're doing a show on Saturday about monsters, do you want to be on it?'

At that time I was a bit overweight, and Alastair is not the essence of tact and diplomacy, but I did feel he'd gone a bit far. He then explained that what he was looking for was an animal to appear on the programme that was much larger than people would expect it to be. I knew straight away that I had just the thing, an adult female red-eared terrapin. People normally think of terrapins as those tiny, green, bright-eyed creatures, about the size of the old half-crown, that are sold in their thousands every year in pet shops up and down the country. But this one had grown to its full adult size of about ten inches long.

Terrapins, along with tortoises, must fall into the category of the most ill-used animals available for sale over the counter. Fortunately, the tortoise trade has been greatly restricted since January 1984. Similar legislation for the terrapin is long overdue. Most people who buy a terrapin have no idea how to take care of it and the poor creature dies a slow, lingering death, only to be replaced by another one. I'm sure few people realise that the tiny thing they buy should reach the size of a dinner plate within a few years if it is looked after properly. Alastair agreed that this would make a worthwhile item for *Saturday Shake-Up*, and the terrapin and I duly made our appearance, however brief, on that week's programme.

A medium once told me that I had a man in a blue uniform watching over me as my guardian angel. He certainly made the trip with me on that Saturday. My luck was in and the piece that I did with the terrapin worked so well that it was used as part of a compilation video to be shown to children's television producers from all over the country at their Annual General Meeting. If you remember the very early days of Independent Television, you'll remember a station called Rediffusion. In the days when everything was live and your hosts for the evening wore dinner suits and dickie bows, and everyone was terribly posh, the first lady 'announcer' to grace Rediffusion's screen was Muriel Young. She is a very attractive, fine-boned lady, with a wonderfully articulate voice and a fantastic memory, which enabled her to recite page after page of the *TV Times*, without the benefit of modern day autocue, to fill in the long gaps between the programmes and the commercials. For many years, she graced our screens in her wonderful cocktail dresses, entertaining and enthralling viewers of all ages, particularly the children when she did her twice-weekly slot with Pussy Cat Willum and Ollie Beak and Fred Barker in *The 5 O'clock Club*. After leaving her position in front of the camera, Muriel went on to become a greatly respected producer of pop programmes and children's programmes in general.

At this time, she was in charge of the children's output for Granada Television and was in the process of putting together a new series called *Graham's Ark*. This was to be transmitted at prime time on children's television, right across the network. It was presented by Graham Thornton and the subjects were many and varied, but each week it tried to concentrate on one particular animal.

Muriel had been frantically searching for someone to co-present a terrapin programme. Graham's function was to be the interviewer, but as he had little personal knowledge of the animal world, she contacted me and we arranged to meet. Almost immediately, we established a rapport and since then we have become great friends.

Muriel is a rare breed of television person, extremely

giving of her time, experience, knowledge and advice. She has taught me an awful lot and I will always be in her debt.

As soon as Mu arrived at the cottage, she realised that this was a likely source of more than one programme for her new series, and before long we'd agreed that I should be involved in three of the first thirteen shows. One was to be on the subject of terrapins, another on tortoises and the third on exotic aviary birds.

If you're ever asked to have a television crew come to your home to make a programme, let me give you one or two words of advice. Don't bother cleaning up. I went berserk with a duster. I cleaned all the windows, I worked myself to a standstill, only to find out that by the time things are lit with those enormous lights they use for television, everything looks great anyway! Also, be prepared for something resembling the Normandy landings. You may be naive enough to think that a television programme is made with a cameraman, an interviewer, perhaps, if you're really astute, a soundman – but that's only the beginning. My tiny cottage was invaded by an army of twelve.

It took me a couple of years working in television to figure out what everybody did. Thank God for my wonderful neighbours. Marjorie and Douglas threw open their farmhouse, and with her usual supreme efficiency, Marjorie catered for all and sundry at the drop of a hat. Marjorie's cooking became renowned throughout the crews of Granada Television, with people volunteering to come back for future programmes, just to taste more of Marjorie's delicious homemade cakes.

It was at one of these feasts that Mu got an idea for yet another programme. At this time, Marjorie's youngest son, David, was a very young fourteen years old. He'd not yet discovered girls and his burning passion was breeding different varieties of hens. These he showed regularly around the country fairs, not without success. One day when we were all sitting around the huge table in the farmhouse kitchen, David entered and announced that he had just won the trophy for the best junior cock. Naturally, not being country folk, the whole crew fell about laughing, thinking he'd been exhibiting himself at some kind of quaint country

fertility rite. Mu was the first to spot the real source of his
pride and invited him to take part in a programme all about
showing hens.

Years later, I had a burglary at the cottage and the loss
which distressed me most was the videotape of David sham-
pooing his hens and meticulously drying them with Marjorie's hairdryer in readiness to secure another rosette. It had
been my evil intention to keep this tape and show it to
everyone on his twenty-first birthday. It's probably just as
well that I no longer have it or I might have made an enemy
for life.

The second fully networked animal programme that I did
for television was to be filmed at my cottage and dedicated
entirely to tortoises. I've always loved tortoises and I originally had two or three, but as usual with my animal collection, people find out that I've got a certain animal and say
do you want this one, so-and-so doesn't want it and it just
builds up. So for the last few years I've had a steady collection of ten tortoises.

We were planning to shoot the programme right in the
middle of summer when the tortoises are at their most active.
We set up a special enclosure in the garden that was the
right sort of area and at the right angle to be filmed and we
built a special tortoise-proof fence and a tortoise house so
that people could see what keeping a tortoise entailed.
However much preparation you do it's never exactly what
television wants and you have to move it round to a different
angle or alter it so that it's quite wrong really but it looks
right on camera – they always say it 'looks right on camera'
– anyway, we had done all this and set everything up and
the garden looked fabulous.

It was the height of summer: all the bushes had leaves on
and the grass was really lush and green, there was plenty
of natural food growing in the tortoise patch for the tortoises
and everything seemed perfect. The camera crew arrived like
an invading horde across the Pennines from Manchester.

I was still new to it all and expected the director to sit
there in one of those chairs with his name on the back
shouting things like 'Action' and 'Shoot' and 'That's a wrap'.
I've only got a tiny cottage and I just couldn't fit this coach

load of people in. Fortunately the weather was superb so we ate and did everything out in the garden.

The day went on and the tortoises performed admirably. They mated on cue and did all the things that people who have got no experience of tortoises don't expect them to do, like charging around and making lots of noise and fighting. It was fabulous and the director was ecstatic. Everything worked well and when we finished for the day and they all went shooting off back to Manchester and that was it. The whole programme in the can, wonderful.

A few weeks later I got a phone call from Mu to say that there had been a problem in the laboratory that was processing the film and that half of the film had been botched up. It just was not workable, and she said that we would now have to arrange another day to come and fill in the gaps.

Of course, nothing is straightforward. If you are going to film something for television you never seem to film the beginning at the beginning and work through to the end. You do all sorts of bits in a different order and so it wasn't that half the film was no good so we could do the second half of the show. They wanted a bit where the tortoise did that and then they wanted a bit with so-and-so and so-and-so, and there is this wonderful thing in television and films called continuity. That means that if you see somebody in a film bite into an apple, and then you see the person they are talking to, and you go back to the first person who has only the apple core left in his hand, that's bad continuity. He should have been given another apple with only one bite out of it. So, of course, continuity had to be maintained for the rest of the tortoise programme. That would have been fine if they could have come within the next month or so when the garden looked much the same and the tortoises were still fighting fit and willing to mate at the drop of a hat. But, again, union problems reared their ugly head and there was a dispute at Granada with some branch of the union and they were on an overtime ban.

What this meant was that if the camera crew set off from Granada Manchester to my cottage which is on the Durham-Yorkshire border, then by the time they had driven from

Manchester to my cottage and had their statutory tea-break on the way, it would have been time to break for lunch and as soon as lunch was finished it would have been time to set off back so that they had time to stop for the statutory tea-break and get back to Granada in time to clock-off. So, in other words, they wouldn't be able to do a thing all that day as far as filming was concerned.

They booked a day in advance for me to do a re-shoot and the union dispute was still on, so I was more than happy because I was being paid a full day's rate for this and I wasn't doing anything. The union dispute continued and another date was booked and duly came and went and I was paid again. It was getting to be quite a profit-making exercise for very little effort on my part. The only problem was that as far as continuity was concerned it was becoming disastrous. Even union power can't do much about the oncoming seasons, and autumn arrived.

With the arrival of autumn came the disappearance of the leaves and by now the garden bore no resemblance to the time when we had actually done the programme. As for the stars of the show, the tortoises, they were ready to kip. They were most uninterested in the fact that Granada wanted to come and continue filming them in their starring role. It was hibernation time and that is what they wanted to do. Eventually Granada contacted me and said the union dispute had been settled, and they had a definite date when they must come and get the rest of the programme in the can, otherwise they wouldn't have anything to transmit and the series was just about to go out on network television.

We had the major task of all time to make the garden look exactly as it was when we were filming. I had to keep the tortoises awake by giving them artificial heat and light in the animal room and keep them feeding and keep them interested in each other. The biggest problem of all was my personal continuity. My lovely lady who does all of my washing had since washed the tee shirt that I wore for the programme several times and it appeared to me to be one or two shades lighter than the original, so I had to scour the shops – by this time in the middle of winter – looking for a tee shirt that was exactly like the one that I had originally worn for the programme. That in itself is no mean feat. I'd also had a completely new hair style, so I had to get still shots of what my hair had been like and go back to my hairdresser and get it put exactly the same. Of course, in the height of summer I had had a fairly reasonable tan, but by this time I was white as a ghost, so I had to get lots of false tan and try and duplicate exactly what I had looked like on the day.

The day came to do the filming. The garden was incredible. It looked very impressive, with a few bushes that had been in pots dug into the garden and put in the right place and a few tubs of greenery moved about to the bits that were now bare. It looked remarkably like the original height of summer. The only thing was it was at least fifteen degrees cooler.

Now that was fine for the tortoises 'cos they had been basking under the electric lights that the crew were using. So they were quite active and quite happy and they performed reasonably well as long as they remained under the heat of the lights. It's not so easy for human beings. I had to stand there in my tee shirt, which I had eventually found, and try to pretend that I hadn't got goose pimples on my goose pimples and apart from anything else when ladies are cold they show it, especially with tee shirts on.

It doesn't matter how thick your bra is, you get certain outlines round the end of your boobs that let everybody know that you are either cold or excited and on this day I can tell you I was not excited, I was cold. Apparently in these situations there is a time-honoured solution which I wish I had never heard of because it's agony. You have to stick elastoplast over your nipples. Putting it on is fine – taking it off is another story. I'll never forget the end of that day. Oh, it brings tears to my eyes just thinking about it.

Anyway the programme went very well and the remarkable thing was, when it was all edited together and transmitted, I couldn't spot the joins. The editing was so good that I didn't know where and when the original bits started and finished. It was one of the programmes that inspired the biggest mail response from viewers desperate to find out more facts and information about the tortoise. It was a great experience and as a result I became heavily involved in a second series and eventually I ended up being given my own series called *Wincey's Pets*.

I will never forget the day when Mu phoned me to offer me my own series. It was just about as good as somebody ringing me to say I had won the pools. I couldn't have been more excited and amazed and astounded and overjoyed and every other fantastic adjective you can think of. I practically did cartwheels round the garden. I must have spent about fifty pounds on telephone calls, ringing everybody I knew just to share my good news.

Whenever anyone rings me and says can you do so-and-so, I say 'yes' straight away and then worry about it nearer the time. I've done this all my life and it has sometimes got me into a lot of trouble. Of course, as soon as Muriel offered me the series I said, 'Wow', 'Great', 'Fantastic', that sort of thing. It was to be seven programmes, and Muriel wanted to call the series *Wincey's Pets*. It would be for pre-school children so it would be on at lunchtime and would feature a different animal for each of the programmes.

Programmes for pre-school children are totally different from any other kind. Young children can only concentrate on any one thing for a very short time, so you have to do things in short, sharp, interesting bursts and the programme mustn't be too long. A maximum of ten minutes or so is about the time that people find the children can maintain their interest.

Muriel and I put our heads together and we decided to do the programme in two halves. For half of the programme I would have an animal in the studio, introduce it to the children and talk about its basic care. In the second half of the programme I would read a story featuring that animal, using cartoon-type graphics in the background; the story would have a bit of fun and a little bit of education thrown in as well.

I had never done anything like that before and I had never read stories on television. I had done a little bit of work on radio but television is another kettle of fish altogether. With television every mannerism seems to be emphasised and I didn't want to be the sort of talking-down person that I got so sick of watching on children's television in my own youth. So we tried to make it fun and interesting. The whole series was to be shot in Granada's studio in Liverpool over a period of two days. I had never been there, but then that sort of thing had never bothered me before.

After several weeks of consultation with Mu, deciding which stories we were going to do and how they were going to work and which animals we were going to feature, it then dawned on me that I had come up with these great ideas but that I had to get the animals to the studio. We had arranged to borrow a couple of puppies and a couple of kittens from a local pet shop, but the rest of the animals it was down to me to supply. At the time I had a very old Austin 1300, two tone beige and rust, and I had to set off from my side of the country to go over to Liverpool, crossing the dreaded M62 with a car absolutely crammed pack to the roof with something to do with animals and the animals themselves.

One of the creatures I was taking for the programme was Molly, my citron crested cockatoo. Molly is a real character and she has since done a lot of things on television. She is a great performer – she likes to show off and she was very excited about getting in the car and going off on this journey. When she gets excited she sometimes starts to scream and this scream is the most ear-piercing noise I have ever heard in my life.

If someone were torturing me to get some information out of me, they would just have to record Molly's scream and play it back into my ears via earphones. I would tell them anything. I think thirty seconds would be the maximum before I cracked totally, quivered like a jelly and spilled the beans. I would be absolutely useless as a secret agent. Molly was in the car, so I couldn't open the windows and I had that nerve-racking feeling of setting off to go somewhere totally new to do something completely new. I was entering uncharted territory, and I am as good at map reading as Billy Connolly is at diplomacy. I'd had the collywobbles for weeks, I hadn't been sleeping well, I had butterflies the size of jumbo jets going round in my stomach and just as I was setting off towards Liverpool, Molly decided to scream. She screamed most of the way down the A1 and by the time I got on to the M62, I was a quivering wreck. I just could not cope with it and decided that Molly could not stay out of her box any more; she had to go into her box and into the boot of the car. Once Molly is in the dark she stops screaming and stays quiet, but I am reluctant to carry her in the box for any long periods of time because it must be quite unpleasant for her. However at this point my welfare had to come before Molly's, so in she went. I closed the car boot and it was reasonably peaceful from then on.

Halfway across the M62, I pulled into the motorway services for petrol. My car looked absolutely ridiculous: every available space had a cage or a bit of equipment in it. I thought I had better open the boot and check on Molly. At that point somebody pulled up alongside and said something to me about the car. Apparently I had been driving along with the seat belt hanging out of the door on the passenger side. I went round to open the door and put the seat belt back in. The boot was still open and a voice came from the boot, 'Hello Daddy, Daddy, hello, hello.' The man's face was an absolute picture. He looked at me, looked at the car, looked back at me and completely ignored it. He had obviously heard it. I don't know whether he thought I was a travelling ventriloquist, but he didn't say a word.

I put in the petrol, he put in his. I went back into the service station to pay, came back out. I sat in the car just sorting things out before I set off. He came back, got into his car, said something to his wife, glared out of the car at me and drove off. I don't know what he said but I do hope that he saw the programme later and realised that I wasn't as crazy as I seemed.

The major problem was having only two days to shoot seven programmes. For the uninitiated that might sound like a doddle. Seven ten-minute programmes – two days – a piece of cake. But it's not that easy and we really had to jam things in. There are so many things that you have to think of beforehand. The programme that really epitomised the whole series of problems that we encountered was the one we did about puppies.

We had two puppies in the studio, a rough collie and a

golden retriever, and they were fabulous. All young creatures are wonderful: my heart warms to them all whatever
they are – baby snakes, whatever. But puppies are particularly wonderful. We borrowed them from a local pet shop
to save hauling things from one side of the country to the
other. I had already done a good impression of Noah. It was
like an ark on wheels with most of my own animals, without
trying to take puppies along as well.

When you run through something in the studio and you
are talking about it to camera, the whole point is that the
director has to follow what you are going to say, so you have
got to decide in advance exactly what you are going to point
to and in which order and rehearse it. On this particular
occasion I had a table in front of me with loads of dishes
containing all the things that are essential to a puppy's well-
being – the different types of food, the vitamin supplements,
the toys that you can get for puppies, the different collars,
all that sort of thing. In rehearsal we didn't have the puppies
there; we just had the table and I went through the order
that I was going to speak about everything. The director
followed me and everything worked like a dream. The
puppy programme was actually the last one in the series
that we were recording; it was the afternoon of the second
day and again union problems dictated that when the studio
crew were due to finish they must finish. They were due to
finish shooting my series at 4.30, so we didn't have time for
things to go wrong.

It was already 3.45 p.m. when we started to do the
puppies. I sat down, the puppies came into the studio and
they decided that perhaps it would be best if I recorded the
story first and then did the puppies second. So, I read the
story, everything went well, lovely story, nice graphics,
everybody was happy. The puppies came: all the dishes
were there, full of different bits and pieces and tasty morsels,
doggy chews and so on.

I started to speak to camera, being quite sincere about the
whole thing, trying to convey, as I felt and do feel, that it is
very important not to take on the care of any animal without
really considering what you are taking on. A puppy is for
life, it's not just for Christmas. If you are lucky it will be

with you for the next thirteen or fourteen years. I was trying to convey this to small children without sounding too patronising and I started to go along the dishes of food and vitamins, etc., in the order that we had pre-designated with the director. As usual the puppies had different ideas.

As soon as they caught sight of the dishes with the food they started to eat. One from one end and one from the other. They were eating too quickly and I was desperately trying to talk quicker than they were eating so that I could get to a dish while it still had something left in it and the director could film something. I was feeling that sort of welling up in my stomach, that sensation of mild hysteria, and thinking, Oh God, the time's running out and we are not going to get this done. The puppies were eating faster and faster.

By this time I thought the puppies were going to burst. The little golden retriever pup looked like a ball with a leg on each corner. I couldn't appear to be too forceful in restraining the puppies or we would get thousands of letters saying Wincey Willis was cruel to the animals on television. I was looking straight into camera, being very serious and saying, 'And don't forget, if you have got a puppy don't leave it for a long time unattended, make sure that you watch what it is doing. Don't let it get into situations where it could get hurt' and just at that point there was an enormous bang and the golden retriever fell off the table. It bounced. It had eaten so much it didn't even feel itself hitting the floor but that was the trigger. I started to laugh, the cameraman started to laugh and the whole place erupted. It was that kind of infectious hysteria that goes round a room when everybody knows that time is running out and you have got to get this thing done and you have no choice, it just *has* to work.

Eventually we calmed down enough to finish the piece with literally two minutes left. I have never been so drained and so exhausted in my whole life, and I don't think that the puppies ate for a week after that programme, though I'm sure they must have been ill from it. They were bursting at the seams but there was really very little I could do at the time to stop them.

This is the sort of thing that can always happen when you are working with animals in television. Although that programme was recorded, the time was running out and we were under almost as much pressure as if it were live. That's half the joy of it really – the animals are totally unpredictable and you just have to cope.

After doing some animal programmes for Granada, I was on a visit to Tyne Tees Television. They had, unbeknown to me, been looking for someone to present the weather. Unlike the BBC, who use members of staff from the Met Office, they wanted a 'personality' weather presenter. They had auditioned quite a few people but had not found what they were looking for. It was suggested that I should try for the part, although I explained that I knew absolutely nothing about the weather. I was told that was of no importance – the weather information would come from the Newcastle weather centre. What they wanted was someone to deliver it. Before the audition I was terrified. They promised me a forecast which did not materialise. Later I discovered that it was an old trick to see if you could cope under stress. I would hate to see a recording of the audition – it was dreadful – but I got the job. I'm sure what did it for me was the fact that it was the very day before the royal wedding of Charles and Di. I did a mock forecast for the street parties that were to be held throughout the region. I said I knew it was going to be a lovely day because apart from the Met forecast and the satellite picture, my mother's knee hadn't been aching all week.

June

Nearly Midsummer's Day. Doesn't time fly? A time when the ancient Celts lit bonfires to worship the Sun God. On the following day men and beasts were said to pass over the ashes to ward off disease and ill luck. I'm glad we don't still have to do that. I can't imagine many of our beasts revelling in a procession over the embers, not to mention Malcolm. By now Malcolm is already turning brown at every available moment – he does his own bit of Sun God worshipping. Makes me sick. After one day I look like a well-cooked lobster and he looks like the Italian waiter serving it.

It's a season to be out of doors as much as possible . . .

In the middle of feeding the animals at the far end of the garden, I heard the dogs start to bark, which sent a message like jungle drums through the rest of the creatures. As soon as the dogs bark, the cats scatter in all directions, which then sets the macaw off screaming. This in turn is picked up by the rest of the parrots, finally reaching me at the top of the garden with the rapid disappearance of Kentucky the demented cockerel. Someone was obviously at the front door. I think it would be virtually impossible to arrive at the cottage unannounced. I went down to investigate and discovered a middle-aged man in the immaculate uniform of a travelling salesman. He looked quite out of place in his smartly pressed suit, white shirt and sober tie. He was holding a small cardboard box. I always greet this sight with a mixture of excited anticipation and dread – excitement that the box may contain something I have never encountered before and dread that I may discover something so badly injured that I can do nothing to save it. Fortunately on this occasion, the excitement was justified and the contents of the box seemed perfectly fit. It contained one of our more interesting summer visitors – a swift.

Swifts conjure up balmy summer evenings as they sweep the skies, constantly feeding on the wing. Many people confuse swifts with swallows or house martins. They are in fact relatively easy to identify in flight and actually this is the only way you are ever likely to encounter one. Swifts are the birds with the largest wing span for their size, and broad wings which they need to keep constantly aloft. Unlike the swallows and house martins, they do not have flashes of white on the underside and their tail is much shorter. Once a swift has left its nest, the next time it lands will be a year later, if it survives the long migration, when it returns to nest itself. As swifts spend their lives on the wing, sleeping, eating and mating, they have little need for legs and feet. Evolution has taken its course and the bird which is master of the air is incapable of taking off from ground level if by accident it finds itself in such a position. Its legs and feet have diminished to such a degree that it now only has two sets of claw-like appendages with which it grasps the side of the nest. To facilitate easy feeding it has a very large mouth in relation to the size of its head. As it flies along with its mouth open, the mouth acts as a trap and catches any flying insects. The swift is not the most beautiful bird I have ever seen but, as usual in nature, it is perfectly adapted to its niche on the ecological ladder.

The gentleman said that he had hit the swift with his car only a few miles down the road and was directed to our cottage by one of the local people. He was very concerned about the bird's welfare and despite the fact that he was very late for an appointment had gone out of his way to seek us out. On examination, the bird did not appear to have any major injury but was slightly stunned. It also appeared far too young to have left the nest. I ascertained exactly where he had had the accident, assured him that we would do our best and he went on his way. I put the swift in a hospital cage to recover and jumped in the car to try and find a swift colony anywhere near the place where he had picked up the bird. I saw other swifts in the area and discovered that they were nesting in a totally inaccessible point around the old church steeple.

The best course of action when dealing with an immature bird such as this is to return it to the nest but as this was out of the question, I was already dreading the task which was ahead. I'll never discover the exact reason why the swift had attempted to fly, as it was obviously nowhere near ready to do so. The only thing I could surmise was that the nest had collapsed, which sometimes happens in old buildings. The other possible cause of the swift's premature departure from the nest was infestation of the nest site, a common problem which affects martins, swallows and swifts. These birds return each year to the same nest, which quite often becomes riddled with parasites and on occasions this will drive the demented birds from the nest. However, this particular bird did not seem to be endowed with visitors, so I felt the former reason was the more likely cause. As parent birds make constant visits to the nest with beakfuls of flies to fill the ever-gaping beaks, I knew I had a difficult task ahead if I wanted to finish the rearing of this one successfully.

Hedge-sweeping is an old trick that bird people use to collect a motley assortment of creepy crawlies. I must admit that most people who live in my area are sure that I am not quite all there and this particular summer's activities confirmed it. I became a positive motorists' hazard as people gaped from their cars at this lunatic in the hedgerow. Not many people readily grasped the significance of my worth-while labour, if all they saw was me standing up to my kneecaps in nettles with an open upturned umbrella at the base of the hedge while knocking hell out of the rest of the hedge with a big stick. This action dislodges all the insect life, which falls into the umbrella and then you close it up quickly, hold the top tight and dash off home to make greenfly purée. It was a task which took me a good fifteen minutes, and it would take the swift on the wing one or two minutes to catch the equivalent amount of insects. As a stop-gap measure this was fine, but as a long-term practical idea, it was crazy. I had to find a source of insects somewhere. I contacted a local school and discovered to my relief that the science master was breeding fruit fly and crickets by the thousands and he happily agreed to let me have starting cultures of both. The fruit fly bred in the laboratories are a special wingless variety which are infinitely more manage-able than the sort we are all familiar with flying round any piece of rotten fruit left outdoors for more than a couple of days in the summer months. A combination of fruit fly and cricket seemed an adequate diet for the young swift, who consumed unbelievable quantities every day.

To strengthen his wings he needed to exercise and so each

day while working in the garden I allowed him to cling on to my sweater where he would flap his wings like a clockwork brooch, building up his strength for the massive journey ahead. After two weeks, I felt he was ready to go and late one fine sunny morning I walked out with him to the middle of the large field next door to the cottage. This field has a rise in the middle and I felt that this would be a good vantage point from which to launch him on his airborne life. I had also learnt from bitter past experience that releasing anything you are not quite sure of is best done in a wide open space. If the creature cannot make it, it will be much easier to catch if you don't have to fight through hedgerows or thick undergrowth.

There is always a mixture of sadness and happiness about releasing something back into the wild – you can't help but grow fond of the things you take care of and you are sad to see them go. But happy in the fact that you have achieved that which you set out to do. Then you can only pray that they survive. It was with these mixed feelings that I held my hand aloft and launched the swift on to the warm summer wind. I had miscalculated – after a short flight he came down to earth with a very ungainly landing. My heart almost stopped: it would have been unbearable if I had suffered all that trauma only for the swift to die through my lack of judgement. Fortunately the grass was quite long and the bird was uninjured and not unduly shocked. Back home again, crickets and fruit flies for tea! I would try again later. Over the next few days, his wing exercises became more and more frantic and finally I was in no doubt that he was ready to go. I went back to the same launching pad and waited to see other swifts in the area before once again I gave him his final helping hand.

This time there was no hesitation, he soared off on the first available thermal up-draught and was soon gone out of sight. When finally the migrating birds set off on their long journey to seek the sun, every swift that I watched leave I imagined was him, and when the following spring the swifts returned to the area, I hoped he was among them.

At this time of year there's a lot of activity in the animal world. Lots of births and even more youngsters trying out their first taste of independence. Many birds produce two clutches of eggs each year and in an exceptional year, three, to ensure the survival of the species. It's been estimated that out of a nest of seven young robins, only one is likely to survive to maturity and go on to breed. And, likewise, the tiny blue-tit has often been recorded as rearing as many as fifteen babies in one go, but most of those are unlikely to make it through the first winter.

It's natural for us to think that birds instantly know how to do everything that their parents do, from the moment they venture out of the nest. This is not always the case, and a lot of behaviour is learnt through copying the more experienced birds around. Many unwary youngsters fall prey to that most skilled of domesticated killers, the cat. And thousands die each year in the paths of our speeding motor vehicles.

It's funny the daft bits of information that clutter up my brain, but I would never buy a pale blue car, because I once read that you are much more likely to kill a bird while driving a pale blue car than any other colour. It seems that birds do not notice this colour as readily as all the rest. I wonder if it's something to do with the fact that it's the same colour as the sky and, when in fear, birds instinctively fly up towards that colour and the safety it would normally afford.

One road casualty that came my way was a beautiful tawny owl with a badly broken wing. It arrived on my doorstep, courtesy of a caring stranger, who had found it by the roadside and had been given directions to the cottage. It was a Sunday and this chap had gone several miles out of his way to do what he could for the frightened bird. I do take heart when this sort of thing happens, as all too often we read about cruelty and ignorance where animals are concerned.

Even though it was Sunday, I rang Neville, my lovely tame vet, to ask again for his help. Fortunately, he was just about to leave home to go to the surgery and so he suggested I meet him there within the next half hour. Over a period of time, Neville had developed a technique for dealing with badly broken wings which, when I first witnessed it, looked like butchery of the worst kind, but turned out to be extremely successful. It involved inserting a thin metal rod into both ends of the broken wing and pushing them together, often with the end of the rod protruding right through the joint of the bird's wing. This end piece was then snipped off with a pair of wire cutters when the wing appeared to be in the correct position. I never let on that the first time I helped Neville with this operation, I did feel a bit sick. But curiosity overcame my queasiness and I learned a lot.

We performed this operation on the tawny owl, and while the bird was still anaesthetised, we took a couple of X-rays to make sure that everything was okay. We had just finished when the phone rang with a frantic cry for help from a farmer several miles away. As all country vets will tell you, when the farmer calls for help, it's the very last resort. He'll have tried every known remedy and tested a few unknown ones before paying a vet to use his hard earned knowledge.

The farmer had been waiting all night and much of Sunday for one of his cows to give birth. He'd eventually realised that if something wasn't done soon, he'd lose not only the calf but the cow as well. In the farming world, that would be an unforgivable, uneconomical sin. We jumped into the car and headed off in the direction of the farm. It was a reasonably warm day, so Neville instructed the farmer to hose down part of the yard, feeling it would be better to operate out of doors in the hosed down area, rather than risk the possibility of the cow picking up an infection from the somewhat less that salubrious barn.

I don't know much about cows, but it didn't take an expert to see that she was in a pretty bad way. The farmer was standing in the yard with his jacket off and his sleeves rolled up. His collarless shirt was extremely grubby. He was sweating profusely and his cap was on back to front, a sure sign that a lot of physical effort had recently taken place. I've never seen a farmer in an intact pair of wellingtons. Surely sometimes in their lives they do actually buy new wellingtons, or is there some secret manufacturer somewhere who churns out holey wellies, already caked in the fruits of the farmyard? His cowhand, a clone of the farmer, was leaning against the gate, still holding the calving ropes.

This is one of the tried and tested methods, but on this particular day it had failed to work. For the uninitiated, calving ropes resemble some primitive instrument of torture. They consist of two long pieces of rope with a loop on one end and a piece of wood on the other. The farmer takes the rope, delves into the cow up to his elbow and attaches it to a leg of the calf. He repeats the process with a second rope and another leg. He then uses the wooden ends as grasping handles and pulls like mad. I don't want to come back into this world as a cow.

I've never had any children of my own, but a close friend of mine gave birth to a ten pound four ounce baby boy. When I asked her what it was like she said, 'It was like shitting a row of houses with the chimney pots on.' If cows could talk, I'm sure they'd have something similar to say about calving ropes.

Neville took no time at all to get stripped for action. Jacket and shirt off, he was soon up to his elbow in cow. A Caesarian was absolutely essential and the quicker the better. At this stage, Neville confided to me that the Caesarian was to save the cow, as he felt that it was already too late for the calf. The calf was a monster, similar to a ten pound plus human baby. Neville said this was happening more and more often due to artificial insemination, when the cow had been fertilised with the sperm from a very large bull that under normal circumstances would probably be unable to mate with this particular cow.

He injected the cow and while she was still standing, began to swab down the area on which he was about to operate. His timing was superb. By the time the cow was clean, she was tottering and about to fall. With a slight push from Neville, she fell on her side leaving the ready swabbed side exposed to his skilful knife. It was at this point that I joined in the fray, having already been instructed to remove my watch and scrub down with antiseptic. My job was to sit on her back legs. Apparently it's not uncommon for a cow to kick out under anaesthetic and with that kind of weight behind a kick, anyone in the vicinity would certainly know about it.

Neville later told me of a similar operation when the cow

had kicked him and knocked him unconscious. In true farmer's fashion, the farmer phoned first for another vet to finish the operation and then as an afterthought called an ambulance for Neville.

Neville rapidly cut through the several layers of flesh to get to the womb and, as he probed deeper, instructed me to hold back each side of the incision, so that he could see clearly what was ahead. I'm not a very strong person and I have particularly weak wrists, but it's surprising how adrenalin takes over and you cope with whatever you need to at the time. I was absolutely fascinated and completely in awe of this man who sat on the yard floor, so calmly performing what I considered to be nothing short of a miracle.

The calf was soon extracted, and I felt sure it was dead, but Neville obviously had other ideas. This poor thing was welcomed into the world with a good thrashing, apparently to clear its windpipe. It was then hung by its back legs upside down over the gate, with pieces of straw poked up its nostrils to clear the air passage, and the cowhand was instructed to keep massaging the calf's wet and bloody body.

Neville started to stitch the cow back together again. As I mentioned, his timing was impeccable. He warned me that by the time he'd knotted off the last stitch the cow would be starting to come round and he was right. I was so enthralled with the whole process that I forgot about my instructions to keep sitting on her legs. You only make that kind of mistake once, as I learned the hard way by being propelled half way across the yard, into the unscrubbed section, landing in what is politely known as manure, but on that day was definitely known as shit. At least that's what I yelled on impact. I didn't mind, though, because it was just at this point that the calf started to cough and splutter and join us all in the land of the living. Within twenty minutes of the final stitch being knotted, mother and baby were standing side by side in the cow byre getting to know each other.

I wondered for how long they would have that luxury, or would the new arrival, a bull calf, be destined for the veal market? I've never been able to eat veal.

On cue, the farmer's wife with a rosy face, chapped hands

and a big bosom amply filling her wrap-round pinny, invited us in for tea. Scrubbed down, we joined her in what is normally the only warm place in the farmhouse, the kitchen. The big old kettle was bubbling away on the Aga cooker, which in its time had served as an incubator and wood dryer and was the source of endless supplies of home-made bread and drop scones.

This is the one time when I'm not totally accepted as a country lass: you see, I'm allergic to tea. Ever since I suffered from a serious bout of yellow jaundice, I have been unable to drink tea without feeling sick. There's always a big pot of tea ready in the farmhouse kitchen, but the jar of instant coffee usually has to be searched for. I always get the feeling that people don't think I'm quite normal if I don't drink tea.

When I was working abroad I ate many strange concoctions, so as not to be impolite to my hosts, but I've never been able to get away with drinking tea. I think it's far less impolite to refuse the tea then accept it and then throw up all over the kitchen table. I remember once when I was staying in a log cabin the Black Forest, with a German family, and I was first introduced to muesli. This was in the days before it was fashionable to eat fibre, and I had been used to the traditional eggs-and-bacon-style English breakfast.

A healthy day in the Black Forest started with rising at dawn. That was the only time in my life that I knew dawn existed until I worked in breakfast television. We then went outdoors to bathe in the icy cold mountain stream and set off for a five mile walk, before breakfast!! On the first day, towards the end of the walk, I was starving and really looking forward to my food. I could not believe my eyes when I was presented with a large rough earthen bowl, filled with the sort of stuff that I was used to giving my hamster. It was drenched in goat's milk, which tasted strangely of garlic. Obviously the local goat had been eating the wild garlic plants that were growing in the valley, and whatever you feed a goat, the taste transfers to the milk. To be honest, the mixture looked like I'd already eaten it and I've been put off 'health' food ever since.

We would then spend the rest of the day mountaineering and return home for a supper of sauerkraut. That first evening, I was so hungry that I imagined I could eat anything and I made the great mistake of finishing the whole plateful. It was horrible. But being great hosts, because my plate was empty, they refilled it and I was obliged to repeat the whole process. I should have at least been nominated for an Oscar for my award winning performance. Especially for my encore around the back of the cabin, when I tried to vomit silently. So much for the healthy outdoor life! It nearly killed me.

However, in the farmhouse, I did eventually get my coffee and despite the fact that I stunk like a slurry pit, I managed to eat half a dozen freshly made drop scones dripping with butter. It's funny how you can get used to most things and it seems that farmers have no sense of smell when it comes to the seamier side of their job. I suppose it's like people who work in fish and chip shops ceasing to notice the smell of fish. It was late afternoon by now and we headed back to the surgery, so that I could collect the owl, who was by now fully recovered from its ordeal and was perched, bright-eyed and hungry. I'm always astounded how animals such as the cow and the owl can recover in such a short time from operations which would put the human animal out of circulation for weeks.

I'd been so wrapped up in what I was doing all day that I'd forgotten all about Malcolm who was by now quite frantic. He'd been ringing all over the place to try and find out where I was. At this point I must explain that when it comes to anything to do with blood, Malcolm is totally useless. He's been known to pass out cold when he's heard of someone having a minor nose bleed. Bearing in mind that he had been sitting at home, imagining that all sorts of horrible things had been happening to me, he was not in the right frame of mind to greet me in the state I was in when I arrived at the door. I'd completely forgotten that I was covered in cow blood and, after my excursion across the yard, also a good helping of manure. He took one look at me, his knees buckled and he fell to the floor in a dead faint. Having witnessed this on several previous occasions, I wasn't unduly worried, so I left him on the floor while I put the owl in the aviary, defrosted a dead day-old chick in the microwave, and fed it to the owl, which ate it hungrily. Animal folks have different priorities.

I buy a thousand dead day-old chicks at a time from a local hatchery. They're all the cock birds that they kill off as soon as they hatch, because they're uneconomical to rear. They make an ideal food for birds of prey and for ferrets, but particularly the birds, as they need to consume their food whole, complete with bones and fur or feather. They then regurgitate a pellet of the indigestible parts and this keeps the oesophagus clear. I'm afraid anyone intending to break into my house and empty the freezer would be sorely disappointed. It would be a rare day when they found a side of beef, as it normally contains a thousand chicks, a few pounds of whitebait to feed the seabirds and, not infrequently, a dead bird or two, which I keep either for post mortem or for use in lectures to school children.

Malcolm eventually came round and I had to get changed quickly because the dogs were going potty as they desperately tried to roll up my trouser leg! Have you noticed when you take your dog out, it'll always find the stinkiest pile of something and be on its back in two seconds flat with its legs in the air, gaily self-anointing, as though it had just found an underground spring of Chanel No 5.

While I'd been so busy with Neville, another owl had been brought to the cottage. I'm sure people all over the country who take in injured wild things will tell you that it is rarely an isolated occurrence. More often than not, if you find a bird, you can bet that within the next twenty-four hours or so, another one or two of the same kind will join it. I often wonder if they're all from the same kamikaze family.

This second owl arrived unconscious, but on close examination appeared to have nothing broken. In cases like these, the immediate treatment is heat. I've always got a couple of thermostatically controlled hospital cages at the ready and this owl was put into one at a temperature of 90 degrees Fahrenheit. Within half an hour or so it came round, but it had that dull faraway look in its eyes that bird people everywhere will tell you usually means the worst. And not long after this, it died. When this happens it's advisable to remove it from the hospital cage as soon as possible, as all wild birds play host to hundreds of tiny white bird lice. These parasites live in the warmer parts of the bird's body. As soon as the bird dies and it loses its body heat, the lice move off like rats from a sinking ship, searching for a new source of heat. They can rapidly infest every corner of the hospital cage and it's a hell of a job to fumigate it. They're also not averse to a touch of human warmth and I wish I had a pound for every one I've killed crawling up my arms when I've been dealing with a sick bird. It was quite late in the evening, so I popped the owl into a big polythene bag, full of de-lousing powder, as I intended to give it a post mortem the next day.

On the Monday morning I was feeding the animals and I heard the phone ringing. Why does it always ring when I'm up to my armpits in something foul with a macaw on one shoulder and a cockatoo on the other trying to eat each other, a couple of dogs are bringing me toys to play with and I have a watering can in one hand and a precariously balanced pile of food dishes in the other? Mental note, must remember to ask Father Christmas for one of those phones that you can carry up the garden. Most of the people who know me well know to leave the phone ringing a long time, cos it always takes me ages to get to it. I eventually got there and Mu was on the line. She wanted some help. She had decided after all these years to bring Ollie Beak out of the closet and back on to the TV screen. She'd telephoned Wally Whyton, Ollie Beak's puppeteer, to get the arrangements underway and she'd just had a call back from him to say that when he took Ollie out from the cupboard under the stairs, the moths had been at him and he was nearly bald. Mu didn't think that a skinhead owl puppet would go down too well, so she was phoning me to ask if I would go to the farm and scour David's hen houses to find some suitable feathers to re-thatch Ollie. I said okay, I'll do my best and put the phone down.

When I eventually finished feeding the animals, I set off down to the farm. As it was a particularly warm and dry day, I took a disposable surgeon's operating mask with me. I would advise anyone who keeps birds, especially pigeons, parrots or hens, to wear some kind of mask when you clean them out in the summer. The dust from the birds' droppings has been known to cause serious illness to some people after long-term exposure. I get so used to wearing one in summer, I often forget I've got it on and I've been known to scare someone half to death when I've absentmindedly answered the door like that.

Now David may have been renowned for his prize hens and he may be the proud possessor of the trophy for best junior cock, but he'd never have won any awards for cleanliness and normally the floors of his hen houses resembled guano-covered seabird breeding colonies. But, surprise, surprise! Yesterday had been the day that David had decided to do a complete spring clean. I found out later it was because he was due to host a meeting of the local group of the Fancy Hen Association, and did not want them to see his enclosures in all their normal glory. I would have found more feathers in a foam filled pillow; everywhere was so clean that I couldn't even find a loose feather in the yard.

It was only when I got back to the cottage that I remembered the owl in the polythene bag. 'Waste not, want not,' as my Mum always said. I've never been over sentimental about corpses. I'll stay up all night and work my fingers to the bone to do my best to heal something and I'll cry buckets of tears for an animal in pain. But if everything that can be, has been done and the animal dies, I try to look upon it as another specimen to be investigated from a medical point of view or, if the cause of death is clearly known, in suitable cases the possibilities of feeding it to another animal must not be ignored. I made sure that the owl was completely deloused and then sat down to pluck it. I was halfway through when the phone rang. It was my mother. After talking for a brief while, I explained that I had to dash because I had to finish plucking the owl before lunch. I was always convinced that my mother never really listened to me and since then I have been certain. Unless she thought that we had rather peculiar eating habits. I sent off the parcel of feathers to Mu and the new Ollie Beak was much better than the old one, who had been dressed in bantam feathers. Some creatures reach immortality via very strange channels.

July

When you are working in television you sometimes get involved in bizarre circumstances. I particularly remember on one occasion having to take part in a live children's programme at Central Television. I was there basically to fulfil a child's wish: a little boy had written in and said he wanted to do the weather with me on television. So, we set up a weather board and did a mock weather report but, of course, as usual television wanted two for the price of one, so while I was there they decided to use me for the animal shots as well. That morning they were also fulfilling another child's dream, which was to feed a kangaroo.

There was a full-size kangaroo in the studio. Normally studio floors are covered with a special shiny plastic stuff that can be made to look like anything at the drop of a hat. That's fine on television, it looks great. But, as far as animals are concerned, it is not an ideal surface. And being in a television studio, surrounded by an audience of children, doing a live show, is not the norm for a kangaroo, by any means. I was very aware of all the safety angles involved.

Kangaroos are determined creatures and when they want to go somewhere there is very little you can do about it. This kangaroo was quite unhelpful in many ways. It was obviously frightened and the floor surface was dreadful for it. It was slipping all the time and kangaroo feet slipping in any direction are dangerous. Kangaroos use their hind feet as weapons: one kick can break your leg quite easily.

The idea for the programme was that I would take a plate of apples that had been chopped into quarters and start feeding the kangaroo so that the little girl wouldn't be nervous; then she would join me and feed the kangaroo as well. Remember that this was a live programme, and on live programmes you never have enough time to do anything. You're always trying to squash far too many things into any given amount of time anyway, and, of course, animals can't be told to do things on cue.

We were waiting to go on and right next to me was a table on which the plate with quartered apples had been placed at the ready. Now, in television, one of the main bugbears is that union rules are very, very strict. They have their place and I can understand them, not only from the point of view of keeping someone a job, but particularly on a live show. It is important to know who is doing what and when: if everyone does the exact job they are supposed to do, then everyone is sure that it will all be done at the correct time and if it doesn't get done at the correct time they know who to blame later.

I stood next to this table with the kangaroo and handler, who wasn't really as strong as the kangaroo. We were having problems anyway, because the kangaroo was so frightened, and I was really worried that it might hurt one of the children, not to mention that I was scared that it was going to hurt me as well. I thought it was better for me to stand between the kangaroo and the children. We were cued to go in twenty seconds. I turned around to pick up the plate of quartered apples and in the heat of the moment totally forgot the union regulations. Of course, it was a prop man's job. He should have picked up the plate and given it to me. A look of horror flashed across the prop man's face as my hand touched the plate. I realised and froze solid. At that point the kangaroo kicked sideways and the table just about collapsed. Fortunately it was the prop man who caught it and not me or the whole programme might have been blacked. We rounded up the apples just as we were about to go on. Only then did it occur to me that no-one had found out if the kangaroo liked apples.

At any given time, when you have an animal in the studio, it will do something perfectly in rehearsal, but as soon as the red light is on, it won't. It wouldn't touch the apples, it wouldn't do anything the trainer was expecting it to do and the whole thing turned out to be quite a shambles. No-one got hurt, that was one good thing and I got paid for it so I suppose it wasn't all bad. Later, off camera, the child had a much better chance to meet the kangaroo and returned home with plenty of autographs of the stars.

The other occasion when I had to work with a kangaroo was quite a few years ago when I was in radio and the powers that be in the local radio station decided that it would be a wizard wheeze for me to go and be a clown in the circus for a couple of days. I don't know what they expected to get from this as the circus is rather a visual medium – it's hardly radio but they decided to let me be a clown, so I went along.

I don't know how people work in circuses. Apart from my distaste at some of the animal aspects, I just don't understand how people can put up with the dingy caravans and the dreadful conditions. The romantic image of running away to join a circus went right out the window.

The amazing thing about being a clown is that – I didn't know this until I got there – every clown has his own face. It's like a sort of patent, the clown's trade mark. You're not allowed to duplicate another clown's face. In each circus the senior clown allocates a face to the junior clown and he, of course, knows through tradition and history that there are no other clowns with that particular face. I had gone along with an idea of the sort of make-up that I wanted but that was knocked on the head immediately. I was duly given my clown's face, my big baggy trousers and the whole bit, and we went into rehearsals.

I was due to do three things in the circus. One was what they call the water entrée, which is that scene that you see where the car all falls to bits and water squirts out of every available orifice. Everybody gets drenched: they all tumble about all over the place and eventually the car is pulled off and all the clowns are soaking wet. It is incredibly tightly rehearsed and so very well timed: it looks like a complete shambles but every clown knows exactly which way he is going to fall and when. They count their way through it mentally. You go in counting 1, 2, 3, 4, 5, 6, 7, 8, 9, 10 to yourself and at 10 you fall to your left and he falls to his right and somebody squirts water through the middle. Consequently for quite a part of the rehearsal I got unintentionally drenched because I was counting 10 and falling to my right instead of my left.

When we eventually got all that sorted out and it was going quite well, they said go off and get changed and we'll do the bare-back riding. What? I thought, Oh no! But I put on the usual nothing bothers me face and I went off and changed. When I came back into the circus arena, a huge horse had appeared. I hadn't learnt to ride at that point and when you're standing next to a horse it really can be intimidating. This was an amazingly huge beast, but the one good thing about it was that it had a very broad back. So I thought, well at least if I'm sitting up there I can sort of perch in the middle and I've got less chance of falling off.

They put a huge safety waist band, like a very wide leather belt, around my middle and hooked it on to a rope which was then hooked up into the guide wires in the roof of the big top. On the face of it, it looked OK, with a safety belt, no problem. As soon as I got on the horse, the trainer said go. The horse knew exactly what to do and started to walk around the ring; in no time at all it was cantering. I was sitting on the back of the horse but I wasn't holding myself on: they were keeping the rope taut so that I was poised on the horse as it went around. Then the trainer said to me, 'Right, next time around kneel on the back of the horse' – so next time around I duly did what I was told, I got up on my knees and thought, 'Oh, this is great. It's a doddle.' The horse was going around and around and the momentum was building as it does when you go round in circles, and then the trainer said, 'Right, stand up.' So I stood up and all the time the rope was being pulled up a bit more and kept taut so I was being suspended at just the right height and it was quite okay. The horse slowed down and I slowed down and got off – fantastic, wonderful.

The third thing I was supposed to do was run on trying to stop the kangaroo who was supposed to be a runaway and then one of the clowns would have a boxing match with the kangaroo. The chief clown said to me, 'Hold on to the kangaroo's tail. It knows what to do – it'll go in and pull you round a couple of times and then you skid off next time you come to the entrance and the other clown will take over.' Have you ever tried to hold on to a kangaroo's tail? It is no joke. In a pair of about size 86 trousers, those big things with the hula hoop and the elastic braces, I didn't know where I was. I didn't know what direction I was going in, my trousers came up over my face, so in the end they thought it was best if the kangaroo bit was left out. Fine, that suited me. From an ethical point of view, I didn't particularly want to be involved with an animal act in the circus. I don't really like tigers and lions doing circus acts, and elephants in particular I feel live in appalling accommodation. Horses are different – because they're domesticated and trained, they get a great deal of pleasure out of working with people, so I didn't have too much of a hang-up about working with this one. But generally I think circuses have enough entertainment to offer with the people doing the business rather than the animals.

The big night came. The audience was there, the big top was full and then the circus music started. I was quite excited, I had my face put on by the chief clown and we all ran on – great cheers and all the people from the radio station were there screaming and shouting. We had given out pictures and hats and badges and car stickers from the radio station. It was all going very well. The ringmaster did his introductory bit and I came into the centre of the big top and did a bow. Then they brought the horse out: I did the whole build up, got on the horse and started going round at a canter.

The rope, which had been taut all the time, was going round and round and at the same time the momentum was building. I got to the point where I was kneeling and everyone cheered – it was wonderful, I felt really good. At the given signal I stood on the horse's back and was just about to spread my arms wide and show off like mad when the chief clown yanked the rope right up into the big top. I had been set up. This was totally unexpected. Anything that supports you round your waist is a bit precarious anyway, but when you are suddenly yanked – it must have been fifteen or twenty feet off the ground – supported only by a wide leather belt, it doesn't half shake your dinner up. I'd had an early evening meal and by the time I'd spun round for the eighth time, bearing in mind I was powered by this massive momentum that the horse had built up, I was convinced that the first three rows of the audience were going to know what I had for dinner if they didn't stop it soon. It was that sort of slow motion, long distance thing of looking down, seeing faces staring up, with everyone laughing and screaming, and me physically going greener by the second thinking, 'Oh God, don't let me be sick.' Then

I realised why I had the clown's make-up on, it was to disguise the nauseating colour that I was underneath it all.

Eventually I was lowered down into the ring and I thought I had been split in two. I was in agony. The leather belt had dug right into my side and several years prior to this I had had an accident at a fun fair and had broken a couple of ribs and at this point I was quite worried that I was in physical danger. They helped me stagger out of the big top and I was allowed to rest long enough to get myself together and into my other outfit to go out and do the water routine.

They put the huge rubber sheet on to the floor of the circus ring, and we all came out. It went extraordinarily well. I was amazed because I had been feeling so nauseous after the horseback riding. I was surprised that I remembered when to count and where to fall. Everything worked well and it looked fantastic and at the end of it we all ran out waving. The rubber sheet on the floor had collected puddles as the water was flying in every direction, and I was getting so enthusiastic that I went skidding out towards the exit, one foot went from under me and I fell flat on my back. Everybody thought it was a great exit, all part of the plan, and they cheered and clapped wildly. I was bruised from head to foot.

We all ran out to the cheers of the crowd. In rehearsals I had had plenty of time just to go sedately into a caravan and change. I hadn't thought about what would happen on the night. It was dark outside and very, very cold and we were all soaked to the skin. A large furniture van with the back end open was backed up to the entrance of the circus flap and all our dry clothes had been laid out in it so that we could get dried and changed quickly and not catch pneumonia. Suddenly I froze and realised that I was the only woman amongst five clowns, one of whom was a midget, a wonderful little guy. They all simultaneously realised the position. We stopped and looked at each other, dripping wet, absolutely freezing. The midget – his nose was at the height of parts of me that whether they were wet or not I wasn't going to let him see – blushed right through his clown's make-up and you could see it to the roots of his hair. For about five seconds we all stood and stared at each other. Then somebody's teeth started to chatter and I said, 'Oh sod it' and started to strip off. We all huddled in corners with our backs to each other and quickly got into our dry clothes. It was certainly an interesting experience, but I don't think it's one that I would like to repeat.

July is a lovely time of year, with some of the best weather that we are likely to get. All the birds in the garden aviaries look fabulous in the sunshine, sitting proudly on their perches, a lot of them with their offspring at their sides. Loads of mock fighting goes on between neighbouring birds, which usually doesn't end in anything serious, but it's always advisable when building aviaries to put double wire in between each aviary flight. It's a noisy time of year with a lot of the youngsters finding out that they've got voices too and the tortoises, who are out in the garden by now, can create a hell of a racket. Most people don't realise that tortoises are very noisy lovers. It's not only the sound of shell hitting on shell, but at each amorous thrust the male tortoise opens his mouth wide and gives the nearest thing to an orgasmic yell that tortoises can manage. When you've got a few of them in the garden doing this, it can be heard from quite a long way off. Sometimes it seems there is very little else going on in my garden but frantic bonking. It's like a day trip to the red light area of Amsterdam.

It's also now that I'm able to feel safe leaving the terrapins outdoors. Terrapins are the Houdinis of the Chelonian world. It's fantastic the way they can climb over quite high wire netting and fall down the other side, without apparent injury. Let's face it, if you were designing a climbing machine, you wouldn't be very likely to start with a large round rigid shell and an appendage sticking out of each corner. I thought I'd made the Colditz of terrapin enclosures – nothing was going to get out this time. But after two days, I was one terrapin short, an adult male of the European pond variety. I'm always worried when I lose an animal and particularly in this case, as European pond terrapins are becoming quite rare. He was one of only two males that I had to mate with my seven females. However Casanova-like these animals tend to be, I felt it was pretty unlikely that my one remaining male would manage to keep seven ladies happy.

I searched high and low for him, but as the cottage is totally surrounded by farm land and, at this time of year, the crops are nearly as high as the proverbial elephant's eye, I didn't hold out much hope. On the rare occasions when this sort of thing happens, I've always found it a good policy to make it known to my local network of village children that a reward is waiting for the finder. After two weeks I'd given up hope of ever seeing him again when I got a phone call from someone in a village two miles away to say that her neighbour had found a tortoise and had I lost one? I took the details and went along to see the lady, hoping that I'd be able to persuade her to allow me to add this tortoise to my group, as I'm always distressed when I hear about people keeping one of anything on its own. She led me into the backyard where she'd made a small enclosure and had done exactly what most people would do on finding a tortoise – put some lettuce down for it. Lettuce is about as much good as a piece of cardboard, if you're considering it as a staple diet. In fact it's probably less use than cardboard – at least eating cardboard you might feel full. Lettuce is about ninety per cent water and very little else of use. However, this tortoise had stoutly refused to eat anything. And when the lady lifted it out from its little shelter, it was very clear why.

The 'tortoise' was in fact my wayward terrapin, who had been found walking along the road in the middle of the day one and a half miles away from my cottage and ten days after it had escaped. The poor thing was totally dehydrated, as it had not had access to water at all and normally it would spend about seventy five per cent of its day swimming and hunting for its food. When I explained what it was, she was very apologetic and went to great pains to excuse her ignorance, which was totally unnecessary as she had done the best she could. At least she'd stopped and picked it up, whereas I'm sure many people driving along that road had already ignored it and a few of the wrong sort would even have used it as target practice.

All creatures of a reptilian nature are marvellous survivors.

Terrapins in particular take a long time to die. I suppose it is due to their ability to slow down their body functions. It didn't take long for this one to improve, and within five days it was again seeking the affections of the ever-willing females.

I'm positive most of the hedgehogs that we see squashed on our roads could have been avoided with a little bit more care. I digress again, but I don't think a lot of people realise what a friend a hedgehog can be to gardeners. The decline of this beautiful little animal has not only been due to careless motorists, but also to the careless use of poisons of one sort or another that people seem willing to scatter about their gardens with the gay abandon of a confetti thrower at a wedding – please don't use slug pellets. I know slugs can be a dreadful menace, but the best way to get rid of them, affording no harm to any other creature, is to sink a shallow dish into the soil every couple of yards or so along your border and fill it with beer. Slugs can't resist a tipple. You'll soon find it full of drunk or drowned slugs that are very easy to dispose of.

Another great hazard for the hedgehog is the garden pond. I think if you've got a garden, a pond is a wonderful thing to have. But please build it with shallow sides. This enables creatures to get out easily if they happen to fall in. My neighbouring farmers get a really good laugh when they see me on my hands and knees at the various cattle grids in my neighbourhood. These man-made structures often fill up with water and are death traps to hedgehogs who spend a long night drowning. I go around building stone stairways so that the hedgehog has an escape route. I don't care if my neighbours think I'm crazy, hedgehogs don't.

August

It's nearly time for my birthday. This is my time of year. I always remember when I was a child, all my birthday parties were held outdoors on a long trestle table with a birthday cake baked in the shape of the number of my age, with lots of other children around and even more animals. Isn't it funny how the weather always seemed to be good when you were a child? As I'm somewhat older now, and probably couldn't afford a birthday cake baked in the shape of my age, apart from the fact that it would be a fire hazard with all those candles, I've dispensed with all that. But I do use my birthday to get more useful equipment for looking after the animals.

Even after all these years, my mother still hasn't come to terms with the fact that her daughter could seriously request an incubator to hatch out tortoise eggs as her next birthday present. I'm sure she'd prefer to buy me a nice set of casserole dishes, but then what would someone who hasn't got an oven do with a casserole dish? On second thoughts, some of the heavier ones would make pretty good parrot baths.

One of the nicest things about living in the country is witnessing the obvious changes in the season and if the summer's been good, harvest time is well underway by August. There has always been conflict about townies moving into villages. The incomers, they are called in some areas. Village life is one of the few traditions that is really maintained with ferocity by some locals in certain areas in Great Britain. When we first moved out to the cottage, which is actually about a mile way from the nearest village, we were very conscious that we were the new people in the area. I'd always loved that part of the world and didn't feel a stranger there, as my father had talked about it a lot when I was little. He grew up there and he used to tell me tales about what he used to do, so I felt very much at home going there and I wanted to make sure that we were taken in as part of the area. Really the only way to do that is to muck in and just get down to hard work.

The farming community are some of the most hardworking people in the land. The job is 365 days a year, 24 hours a day. They can't make the lambs be born on a special rota and a work to rule. I know that there are certain chemical inducements now to make sure that the sheep lamb all at the same time, but there are exceptions to every rule. There are always unpredictable things happening and and as long as nature is nature, a farmer's life will be a constant battle. So, we were very aware of trying to become part of the community. It does annoy me a lot when people who have moved out into the country have this image of what it is about from television or from the posh magazines. The sort of green welly and head square brigade who think that as long as you drive a Range Rover and keep a retriever, your child has a pony and you wear a green Barber jacket, have a couple of guns and a gun licence, you are part of the country way of life, well that it a load of rubbish. Those priorities are way down the line and I think the reason we were so quickly accepted into the community was that we did roll up our sleeves and get stuck into work.

We moved in the May and it was hay time and harvest time before you knew it. It was a funny season that year. The weather had delayed the harvest and at the time when Douglas, our neighbour, would normally have had all his sons to help him with the harvest, they had gone back to college. We saw them out in the fields working and just put on our wellies and our scruffy old clothes and went out and said, 'Can we help?' No farmer will ever turn down free labour, and I worked about the hardest day's manual work I had done from the day I was born.

What amazed me then and has never ceased to amaze me every harvest time since is where straw manages to get to throughout the course of the day. By now I've learnt to strip off in the garden – fortunately we've got a back garden that isn't overlooked by anything – and divest myself of all the bits of straw or hay that have managed to worm their way into my clothes. You have a navel full of it. It's in all your secret parts. It's in your ears. It's up your nose. Everywhere you have an orifice straw or hay will find it and it is uncomfortable, but, digressing again, it's part of the joy of the seasons. We moan like hell about it, but it is fun when the harvest all completed – you feel a real sense of achievement.

I knew we had been accepted into the community when,

after the end of the first harvest, we were all down on the farm having tea. By tea I mean the old traditional cup of tea (coffee for me) with jam and bread and cakes and all that sort of thing. Anyway, we were having tea after harvest and Grandpa, who was not an easy man to win over, but fascinating nonetheless, sat and intensely discussed with me the nuisance of these townies that had moved into the village. These townies had lived in the village for five years and we had been there for about as many months, but it seemed that we had been accepted into the community and we've felt very much part of it ever since.

Harvest time brings a lot of work to the farm but it also brings a lot of fun. It's the one time in the year when virtually everyone is all doing the same job or part of the same job and everyone is pulling together. The entire family has something to do with harvest and that first year really opened my eyes to what a large family was like. I always joke with Marjorie that I imagined it would be like having the Waltons as neighbours, with them all sitting around the big table having their meal and saying Grace and being wonderful to each other when in reality, of course, it's nothing like that. The youngest was fighting with the second youngest who was fighting with the eldest and Father was telling them all to shut up and Mother was just closing the farmhouse door and forgetting about the whole thing. But it was a lot of fun.

One of the things that made them all laugh and in fact they still talk about it now, was my attempt at saving anything and everything that lived and breathed from the path of the combine harvester. There was a fine line I had to tread between annoying the farmer, who felt I was putting myself at risk by getting in the way, and trying if I could to stop poor little voles and other creatures from being mangled up in the incredibly frightening machinery that today's combine harvester is. It just chugs relentlessly on, decimating everything in front of it. One day there must have been a nest of voles in the fields – they all scattered in the path of the combine harvester and I was shooing them in the right direction because they are dumb. They often run like mad, then run back and run into the harvester's path again. I was on point duty heading them the right way and one of them, it must have been the smartest vole in town that week, ran straight up my trouser leg. It took me about two seconds to get over the initial shock and then I just grabbed the bottom of my trouser leg, tightened it up round my ankle and then hopped off across the field. I got to the other side and jiggled my leg and the vole ran down and into the hedgerow. It was one of the things, one of the very few things, apart from the inevitable breakdowns, that stopped the combine harvester that year – Steven, Douglas's son, was laughing so much that he couldn't continue. They just couldn't believe this absolute nutcase who would go to all this trouble to make sure that a vole would live to breathe another day.

It didn't take me very long to discover that all the smartest people in television made a habit of thinking up something they'd like to do, inventing a programme about it and getting someone else to pay them to fulfil their dreams. I thought I could do with some of this and suggested to Muriel Young that one of the episodes of *Graham's Ark* should feature the Jersey Wildlife Preservation Trust. For many years I'd been an ardent supporter of the Trust and had taken out life membership.

Long before I ever got into the media, I was mentioned in the Trust's quarterly bulletin for my fund-raising efforts on their behalf. To this day I still pay a hundred pounds a year for the upkeep of one of the parrots in the Trust's collection of endangered species. It's a marvellous place, built on one man's dream and I'm more or less prepared to bet that, as you're reading this, you'll certainly have read one of his books. Don't think for a minute that I'm putting myself in the same class as the marvellous author and true animal man, Gerald Durrell. But as I'm very familiar with animal people and the sort of stuff they read, I should imagine that even my small attempt at putting some of my experiences on to paper would attract other animal lovers.

As you've probably guessed he's another one of my heroes. In fact when I was asked to fill out a form for my inclusion in *Who's Who in Television*, one of the questions was, 'Where would you most like to be when you're not at home?' My answer – the Reptile House at the Jersey Wildlife Preservation Trust. It's the best I've ever seen and I wish I had one like it. As the Trust was just about to launch a special club for children called the Dodo Club, Mu thought that would be a great topic for one of the children's programmes. See what I mean about getting paid to do what you want?

Even though I'd supported the Trust for many years and felt I knew every square inch of it, through the wonderful writing of its creator, I'd never actually been there. It was great to be able to ring Simon Hicks, the smashing man who is the Trust's secretary – only one of the working hats he wears – and tell him that I was going to be visiting him. Not just me: I was bringing a crew from Granada Television to shoot a twenty-five minute programme to be shown all over the country. I was so excited on the day we went and even with all my very high expectations, I was not disappointed.

I am loath to call it a zoo, as that word often conjures up nasty images of animals confined in bad cages, purely as exhibits for the often uninterested human spectator. The Trust was built for the sole purpose of breeding animals that are in danger of extinction in the wild. Gerald Durrell is far-sighted enough to realise that that in itself was not enough, and has set about creating a programme of education, not only for people in this country, but more importantly, for the people who live in the countries where the animals originate. The Trust regularly sponsors animal keepers from all over the world to come to Jersey and take residential courses in the captive breeding of their particular native animal. Gerald Durrell also encourages people around the world to preserve what habitat there is left to enable the release of the animals which they successfully breed.

I was privileged enough to wander round the Trust in the early morning, before it was open to the public. It's a place where the animals come first. Each enclosure is designed individually for its occupants. This of course means that people might have to stand for a long time outside some of the enclosures to catch sight of the animal. If the cage contains an animal that would normally be shy and regularly seek cover, then it will be given adequate cover to make it feel at ease. They even go so far as to plant trees from the animal's native country outside of its enclosure, so that its surroundings are familiar.

At the time that I went with the Granada crew, they were just completing the huge gorilla enclosure. It is one of the largest in the world. At one side of this enclosure there are a series of climbing frames for children to play on. The reason for these being built there might not be obvious to the casual visitor, but the children's antics on these frames are designed to entertain the gorillas. Doesn't that tell you something about the whole attitude of the Trust?

I've since been back to Jersey and seen the family group which occupies this enclosure. Their fantastic breeding success testifies to the skill and care of all concerned.

As I said earlier, I've been paying for the upkeep of one of the thick-billed parrots. When I first adopted this bird a plaque was mounted on the aviary with my name on it. So we thought it was a good idea to start the film on this now very weathered plaque. Opposite the line of aviaries was a newly completed snow leopard enclosure. As the pair of leopards had only just recently been introduced into this, the male was spending a lot of time vigorously marking his territory boundaries. Snow leopards mark in exactly the same way as domestic cats – they point their rear ends and spray. But as you can imagine, there is a substantially larger volume of liquid involved. While we were setting up the shots on the aviary side, Graham Thornton, the other presenter, was leaning on the barrier outside the snow leopard cage. What happened next would have been a certainty for a slot on *It'll Be Alright on the Night*, if the cameras had been rolling. You've guessed it. The snow leopard increased his territory around him to include the reclining Graham.

There are some smells that are almost too foul to describe. Imagine tom cat pee times ten in strength and quantity. He copped the lot. I couldn't do anything for laughing – neither could most of the crew. Mu took over and we eventually followed to find her hosing Graham down in the yard behind the keeper's office. Even when he'd thrown his clothes away and borrowed an overall from one of the keepers, none of us would share a taxi with him on the way back to the hotel.

God knows what the chambermaid must have thought the next day.

Simon Hicks was marvellous and arranged everything to make life easier for us. My one disappointment was that Gerald Durrell was not there, as Simon had told me. When we had finished filming and were getting ready to leave, Simon took me to one side and asked me if I would like to pop up to the house for a quick drink. As the crew were busy, packing away all the equipment, and the good old union regulations wouldn't allow me to assist, I was happy to go for a quick large one or two. He led me into the beautiful manor house around which the Trust is built and we went upstairs to the living area. When he opened the door into the sitting room I couldn't believe my eyes: right in front of me, large as life, was my hero and his beautiful American wife, Lee. I think it was the first time I'd blushed since my early teens, I was so astonished.

Simon explained that he'd had to tell me a little white lie, because Gerry didn't want to appear rude to everyone, but had been working very hard to meet a deadline from his publishers for his latest book. He had just finished as we were packing up to go.

He was exactly as I imagined he would be: a big man with a wonderfully warm smile, a charming manner and most of all, a wicked twinkle in his eye. I sat and hero worshipped for three quarters of an hour, and then I floated back to the hotel. It's so good when you meet one of your heroes and you're not disappointed. And here was little me, managing to help the Trust in the best way possible, by letting millions more people witness the work that they have been doing for the last twenty-six years. I've visited the Trust on several occasions since and have never been disappointed.

On one of my subsequent visits to the Trust, I was again lucky enough to be allowed to go in the morning with the keepers and spend some time getting to know the animals, before the distraction of the other visitors arrived.

In one of the enclosures there were two juvenile orangutans. One had been bred at Jersey and another had arrived as its potential mate from another collection, doing similar work. Orangutans are very intelligent, and it's fascinating to watch them rapidly adapt to using what they find around them to get what they want. One of these orangs developed a skill for making a long piece of rope by twisting bits of his wood wool bedding together. He used this like a fishing rod to catch peanuts that had dropped out of his cage and fallen between the barrier and his bars. He would twirl the wool and flick it until he managed to secure a peanut and then very patiently draw his prize towards him. He also regularly played with the same small piece of stick, a very thin bendy twig which had obviously been left after a leaf-eating session. He used to poke this supple stick into little crevices around his enclosure, where he was unable to put his fingers. I don't know what he was searching for. He played this game for hours on end.

On the last day of my visit to Jersey, I went in the early morning to say goodbye to all my friends, both animal and human. As I stood outside the orang cage, saying my fond farewells, my lovely intelligent little friend came towards me with arms outstretched. I reached out in an effort to touch him as a final farewell gesture. As my hand got closer to his, I saw he was holding his special stick, which he released into my open hand. I took it and then offered it back to him, but he made no move to retrieve it. I've still got it and it's one of the best presents anyone has ever given me.

While working with animals on television, I've always tried to avoid what I call the skateboarding duck type story. These are stories where the animals are usually laughed at and are pictured doing something that is not natural to them. Wherever possible I try to use the time I have on television with animals to educate as well as entertain. However, occasionally, I have been called upon to do one or two crazy pieces that have a novelty value, but are not detrimental to the animals themselves.

One such assignment was to film an animal harvest festival to be held at one of the major RSPCA animal sanctuaries. The enterprising inspector in charge of this centre was always looking for a new angle to raise funds, to get his orphans adopted and to make people generally aware of its existence and the work being done there. He had asked the local vicar to conduct this outdoor service and had invited anyone who would care to to bring along their animals and join in. It was a strange sight when I arrived with the film crew. In front of these stables they had arranged a portable altar and sitting to one side was an old lady playing a portable electric organ. Spread out in front were dozens of bales of straw to serve as congregation seats. All creatures great and small arrived. It was a lovely day and some people arrived dressed in full cowboy outfits, riding beautifully groomed horses. There were people with pets of every kind, from mice to St Bernards. They started by singing *All Things Bright and Beautiful*, and I thought the sound engineer was going to go barmy, with Mabel on the organ, changing the volume after every eight bars, the dogs howling along in the background, not to mention the ducks and the goats. Then the vicar started his sermon. It was at this point that I cracked up. He said, 'Our Lord taught us' but what I thought he said was, 'Our Lord the Tortoise.' I found it very hard after that to do a serious interview with this very well-meaning man of the cloth.

I receive the most bizarre letters from viewers. People send me all kinds of weird things through the post. Sometimes I'm quite worried about what I'm going to find. At this point I'm not talking about the pornographic material which arrives regularly for many television presenters, particularly women. I don't know what to make of that, but I've only ever seen three pornographic letters that women have sent to male colleagues. It's also significant that the recipients seem quite proud, whereas female presenters tend to play the whole thing down. It does make you wonder what goes on behind closed doors. They now have a system of filtering out all that kind of junk before I get my mail, so if you're thinking of getting your pen out of the pocket in your grubby mac, or even worse, sending me the contents of your pocket, then forget it. I have received everything in the post, from the straightforward pornographic polaroid to used contraceptives, but the most bizarre of all has to be the phantom silhouette artist. Do you remember when you were a kid and you used to put your hand on a sheet of paper and draw round it? Well this man gave a whole new meaning to this particular art form. I was sent a series of silhouettes for different stages in the programme of a certain part of his anatomy. He must have been a liar. Surely no-one would need a sheet of paper bigger than A4, however excited he got.

The majority of my letters come from people who want answers to animal problems. Some of them expect a whole book in reply, when all they actually need to do is make the effort to call into their local reference library. Wherever I can, I do try and help and I remember one query that caused me quite a bit of a headache. 'Dear Wincey, Please can you help? Our labrador dog has just bought us a present – do you know the recipe for hedgehog milk?' The immediate answer would be 'No'. But I eventually did manage to track down some useful data and passed on the information. I found that in one of my many reports from the Jersey Wildlife Preservation Trust. They had done some research into the very question, in an attempt to hand-rear tenrecs, hedgehog-like creatures from Mauritius.

September

This time of year always makes me think of Tunisia. At home it is often hot and for a good harvest prolonged dry weather is best. It's the nearest we get to the North African climate I was once quite familiar with.

My first job of any note, at least the first job I really enjoyed, was working as travel courier. It's not so much a job, more a way of life, when you take up a position in your resort – you really are expected to be on duty 24 hours a day, much like a farmer. As long as you are in sight of your holiday-makers they expect you to be able to answer every question, arrange everything they want at the drop of a hat. It was the hardest and most demanding job I have ever done in my life.

For the people on holiday those two weeks were the most important of the year and they had worked the other fifty weeks to pay for them. So, I did try to do my very best to make it as special for them as I possibly could. Having said that – some clients certainly did stretch your good will to its farthest limits and back again. When you do a job like that you really are out on your own – you are living in the resort in the hotel with your customers and they do expect you to have answers to absolutely everything. I don't know what it is about people on holiday: maybe they behave differently because they are in a foreign country and they are not known by the people around them, but they fall into distinct categories. There are those people who, the minute they get off the plane, adopt the character and lifestyle of the person they would really like to be, but, for whatever reason, are not able to be at home. Once they are abroad, they take on this amazing fantasy life, they invent histories for themselves and, usually, create a lot of problems for the courier.

One chap I remember spent the whole coach journey back from the airport making it quite plain, in a very loud voice, that he was not normally the package tour type. He had stayed at all the best hotels around the world. He dropped names like the Hilton in Dubai, stuff like that, and for the first couple of days of the holiday he did nothing but complain about the hotel, the climate, the quality of the service, the food, everything. People always tend to forget that you only get what you pay for, but he insisted that what he was getting was rubbish. In the end curiosity got the better of me and I took his passport out of the hotel safe (the hotel retained passports of all its residents until they had been registered with the police). It was brand new. There was not a single stamp in it, from any country. His occupation was given as 'plumber' and he lived in Bradford. He had successfully managed to disguise his Bradford accent and he had certainly given everyone the impression that he was much more like a high flying financial adviser than a plumber. Once I had discovered his secret, the next time he came to complain (which he did with such frequency that I was beginning to think he was the only guest I had in the hotel), I couldn't resist putting him in his place. He had chosen to complain, yet again, in the middle of a reception. In a very loud voice he announced that his toilet was over-flowing, and I retorted, 'Well, you've complained about the total inefficiency of the Arab workers, I think it might be better, with your expertise, if you had a look at it, then you could give them some advice about how to put it right.'

From that day on, he didn't complain again.

Mostly, though, people are nice. They are out there to have fun and that was what I tried to help them to do. One of the most interesting aspects of the job was to accompany the guests on certain excursions. On the face of it it was potentially quite boring for me, doing the same trip over and over again, but, if you got the right mix of people, it could be fantastic.

The most expensive excursion lasted two nights and three days and included a journey down to the Sahara Desert. I always managed to sell this trip very well and I used quite a bit of psychology to do it. The other couriers, from different countries and different tour operators, used to sell it in the kind of romantic vein – 'We're all going to trek down to the desert to see the fabulous sunsets, the miles of burning sand, the oases and the palm trees' – all that sort of stuff. I knew that, actually, it was very rough, certainly nothing like the image painted in those fabulous desert movies, where the bejewelled Arab prince sits in his tent surrounded by dusky maidens, all offering him bars of Turkish Delight. Nothing could be further from the truth and I told them so. I told

114

everyone that it was going to be the most uncomfortable three days that they had probably ever endured in their whole lives. They were going to be bitten by everything that flew or crawled; they would choke to death in sandstorms; they would risk catching syphilis from the camels (not perhaps the most obvious route via which to catch syphilis, but, in fact, camels are renowned for carrying syphilitic type germs in their saliva). I was not suggesting bestiality, but as camels regularly spat, it was wise advice. I told them that they would encounter cockroaches the size of their fists; the oasis would be a pool of green, rancid water; *but* we would have a good time. I also pointed out that it wouldn't be worth bothering to sign up for the trip unless they were tough and they thought they could hack it.

Of course, that brought out all the pioneering spirit of the mollycoddled holiday-makers and the psychology worked. Those that came did have a tough time, but they had been told that beforehand and they were prepared for it. Inevitably, afterwards, the comments that I had were not complaints, but people saying, 'Oh, come on, it wasn't all that bad, you know. You made it out that it was going to be really tough.' So, it was all very successful. I used to sell half a 42–seater coach and a French courier who had holiday-makers there would sell the other half. Then we would mix the people up. Again, that could be potentially problematic, with a coach load of tourists speaking two different languages. Still, they were all the same type – a little bit more adventurous than the average package tour person – so, they knuckled down, got on and, usually, had a good time.

One incident that really stands out from those trips was the camel ride. We started out from the hotel in a luxurious, air-conditioned coach, with a fridge full of cold drinks, but we were only on it for a few miles, until we got to where the edge of the deserty part of North Africa begins and the road becomes more like a dirt track. Obviously, the coach operators were not interested in taking their high quality coaches on these rough dirt roads, so all the passengers were herded off on to the most dilapidated forms of transport I have ever seen. They were like something out of the wartime era and looked as though they had been through a couple of wars.

To illustrate it more graphically for you: we were driving down a particularly bumpy section of road when the door of the ancient coach fell off. The driver didn't even blink. It didn't phase him for a second, he just drove on. Bits fell about the wayside and, as long as the coach was going forward, it didn't seem to matter. Finally, we got to where the camels were waiting. This was one of those times when none of the couriers ever missed a chance to make some money.

A holiday courier's job is something thousands and thousands of people want to do. They think it is really glamorous and fabulous. Consequently, holiday companies don't need to pay very much to get people to do it. It wasn't a case of looking for the highest salary. It was a case of being paid something, no matter how little, to live in a country, work there and experience the place, without having to fork out yourself. I was on twelve pounds a week plus full board and lodging, which wasn't very much money, but in Tunisia there wasn't much to spend money on. Still, you did need to save, in case you didn't get a winter position. So you took every opportunity possible to make as much extra money as you could. One way was to persuade all your customers that they would enjoy the trip much more if they dressed in suitable clothing, i.e. hired the Lawrence of Arabia type robes from the camel handler, which they all did, with great gusto, and I got a percentage on everything that was hired. The holiday-makers would then climb on the camels and we would pad out across the dunes to an oasis. By this time they would be frying alive, ready to pay anything for a drink.

Wherever you are in the desert there is always an Arab who will pop out from behind a dune and try to sell you something. Arabs never miss a trick. There was one very clever guy who had it all sewn up at this particular oasis. He would be waiting, just as everyone got off the camels, with a big box of ice. I never did find out where he got the box of ice from, but he always had it, stacked full of cool drinks. There were bottles of Coca Cola and an amazing drink called Pschitt, which the tourists found very amusing.

It was spelt Pschitt, but pronounced Shit and they thought that was great. They all took a bottle home as a souvenir but they certainly paid for it, because, by the time they reached this oasis, they were so parched and dying of thirst (even though they had been out in the very high temperature for no more than twenty minutes or so) that they would all pay a pound a bottle for the Coca Cola or the Pschitt. We used to laugh later, on the coach back to the airport at the end of the holiday, when I reminded them they would probably never tell anyone at home how they had paid a pound for a bottle of Pschitt.

The trips out on the camels were really funny, the highlight of the whole excursion. Most of the people had never been anywhere near a camel, let alone ridden one. The camels, on the other hand, were so used to it that they were more or less like the donkeys on Blackpool beach, except that they were somewhat taller and slightly more exotic. Camels kneel down to rest, and you get on while they are in that position. Then, they hoist themselves up in such a way that you are thrown first backwards, then forwards. The reverse happens when you get to the oasis and they stop.

The camel handler, Ahmed, was the epitome of Arab handlers. I don't know whether he was chosen for the post specifically to fulfil the tourists' preconceptions, but he was a very small, wizened guy, with very leathery skin. He wore a very dirty, battered fez and extremely dirty robes. On his feet were knotted rope and leather sandals, which looked as though they had grown with his feet. It didn't appear that he had ever taken them off. He had very, very dark eyes – you could hardly see the whites at all – and the thing which always struck me most was his mouthful of absolutely rotten, black teeth.

There are two things I notice in people: clean teeth and nice hands. If they have both, they're okay. Ahmed certainly had the worst set of teeth I have ever seen.

The camels didn't really need a handler: they didn't have to be told what to do and in fact they had done the trip so often they seemed to be doing it in their sleep. On one occasion we stopped at the camel staging post by the oasis and the camels dropped down on to their knees as usual. One of the tourists was a particularly large lady from Blackpool. She was a really jolly soul, who got into the spirit of everything and even had on her Lawrence of Arabia clothes. I don't know how the camel managed, because she was absolutely enormous. Normally these white robes would be flowing and billowing everywhere, in the hot desert breeze, but on this woman they were stretched taut around her huge body. When she reached the oasis there wasn't really any space left and as the camel ducked down on to its front legs she let out one almighty scream, at the same time propelling her top set of false teeth out of her mouth and down on to the sand. With exquisite timing the camel's rump landed two seconds later and embedded the teeth into the desert.

Trying to explain to Ahmed Ben Ali whatever that he had to get the camel up again, because it was sitting on Ethel's teeth, was one of the hardest things I have ever had to do in a foreign language. He spoke very little French. I spoke very little Arabic. We communicated mainly in sign language and the language that all Arabs seem to understand – money. It was hysterical with me trying to explain that the camel was sitting on Ethel's false teeth and Ethel totally distraught. She couldn't bear the thought of spending the rest of her holiday minus her top choppers and, of course, the rest of the coach party were keeling over on the ground with hysterics.

No one could speak. The tears were rolling down our cheeks. Eventually Ahmed Ben Ali what's his name kicked the camel several times, until it begrudgingly moved forward a bit, so that three of us could start digging down into the sand. Remarkably, we did find Ethel's teeth. As they had landed on the soft sand they were quite unimpaired, although I'll never know how she could have put them back into her mouth, after they had been under that camel's bum.

Another part of the trip that I always remember was visiting the caves at Matmata. These were dwellings carved out of the rocks. Caves make ideal homes, the environment is perfect. So cool and dark after the desert and its dry heat and glare. Nature's perfect air conditioning. If you have seen

Star Wars you will know the caves I mean – they were used as the rock dwellers' homes.

When we were on these excursions, the overnight stops at the different places were quite extraordinary. Tourists had the choice of staying in a bedouin tent, a sort of adobe hut or an 'hotel'. 'Hotel' really had to be said with inverted commas around it: This was several years ago and I'm sure things have improved, but at the time the Tunisian idea of an hotel and ours were worlds apart. I used to warn everyone that it wasn't going to be very special. The nearest this hotel would get to 'Michelin' would be the pile of old bus tyres stacked around the back. The best thing about the place was its population of giant cockroaches and it certainly had nothing remotely resembling adequate plumbing.

On one occasion I was availing myself of the primitive facilities and for once there was a roll of toilet paper. I picked it up and the biggest cockroach I had ever seen fell out of tube and on to my lap. Now I know that I am an animal lover but cockroaches have never been in my all time top ten. I didn't need that kind of a shock – I was already suffering from the runs, or the Tunisian trots as they were known, and if I hadn't been having such a problem I would just have discovered an instant cure for constipation.

Sad sights haunt me from those excursions into the desert. I can still picture the children standing on the edge of the dirt track displaying their merchandise. This consisted of various members of the reptile family that they had caught for the pot. I do realise that to keep anything you intend to eat in any kind of fresh state in that climate, you must keep it alive. However, the sight of these forlorn animals with their legs tied across their backs, baking in the sun, always disturbed me. People did seem remarkably insensitive to the welfare of animals. I suppose if you don't have a very pleasant lifestyle as a human being then your values for the so-called lower forms of life become even more diminished.

It was certainly one aspect of living in Tunisia that I detested. The treatment of the working animals seemed to me not only appalling, but quite stupid from a purely economic point of view. Tiny, half-starved donkeys were quite common. They regularly grazed on the Spartan scrubland, but instead of being tethered by a halter, they were hobbled. This horrific practice meant that a length of very rough rope would be tied tightly around one front leg and then a short length would be left before the other front leg was tightly fastened too – so the poor creature had to shuffle to get around. The rope was so tight that the animal always had open wounds where the ropes had dug into its flesh. These wounds were constantly infested with flies. When the donkeys were released from this torture they would be laden down with goods and a person to haul from A to B in the searing heat. The owner, often weighing more than the donkey, seemed to beat the poor animal irrespective of its performance. It was as if he was humming an imaginary tune and beating the donkey in time to the music.

The most shocking thing that I ever saw, and the picture is still as vivid today as it was then, happened on one of my visits to a remote village. I turned a corner and came upon a butcher's shop. The sign for a butcher's is the head of a freshly killed animal hanging outside. What I didn't realise was that they actually did the killing on the spot. As I turned the corner I saw a sheep standing outside the shop. Just as my eyes met the sheep's the butcher slit its throat. Blood stained the surrounding earth as the animal dropped to the ground. I added to the mess by vomiting. I had nightmares about it for weeks. I can understand the importance of keeping the meat fresh and that is their way of doing things. But to our very cushioned western eyes it was a horrible sight to see.

I think most people have got so used to seeing joints of meat, pre-packed in polystyrene trays and covered in cling film, on supermarket shelves, that they tend to forget it once lived and breathed. Having said all that, I am not a vegetarian. I did try over a period of several months. I went through a moral dilemma, as I'm sure most animal lovers do. I have great respect for anyone who can stick to such a regime. I found that it was impossible for me. I am not a very good cook and I found I was trying to exist on totally unbalanced meals. To do it properly I felt I must give up using all animal products. The life of a vegan is not for me. I endeavour wherever possible to eat produce of the more humane farming techniques. I know that I will receive thousands of arguments to the contrary having written this, but I'm a conservationist above all. Thank goodness the band of like-minded souls is growing daily. Extremes of any kind tend not to work for the cause but alienate those people who are not quite for or against, and I realise that a lot of the animals that are bred now for the meat market wouldn't exist at all if the meat market didn't exist. What I am against and what I endeavour never to encourage is any form of factory farming, whether it be battery hens or any of the other horrific practices that are done in the name of economy – and I wouldn't eat veal or pâté de foie gras to save my life.

But I am digressing again, let's get back to Tunisia, and to some of the other practices which I found quite hard to stomach. The local boys would set traps and catch some of the tiny songbirds: they would catch one bird, tie its little spindly leg round with cotton and fasten it to the ground. When it was calling in distress other birds would flock down to it and they would trap them and keep them in empty food tins. These tins were the size of a small tin of peas with the lid taken off completely. They'd just pop the songbird into it and close the top as you would crush an empty beer can and they used to carry these poor creatures around like that, presumably until they sold them or the birds died. I used to spend a fortune buying the birds from the kids and releasing them. I don't know how many I managed to save but even if it was only half a dozen, it was worth it.

I don't think that I would have managed to survive living in Tunisia for so long if I hadn't had Malcolm with me. We were not married then and he couldn't get any kind of work permit at all. He came out and worked on saving my sanity. Malcolm is the world's best sunbather. He can spend hours just baking in the sun reading a book, absolutely pouring with sweat at the hottest times of the day and show no ill effect whatsoever. I get irritable after twenty minutes and want to do something and I certainly cannot read in the sun, it gives me a violent headache. I have to put my umbrella up but Malcolm can sunbathe with great expertise. In fact it got to the point where he couldn't sunbathe at normal sunbathing times of the day and had to wait until the sun was at its hottest before he even felt any effect. He used to wear a burnous – one of those big black cloak-like garments that the Arabs just sling round to cover everything in the evening – and because he was so dark he was often chased off by the hotel garden guards when he tried to go back to the hotel at night. He used to have to explain that he was English and the only way that he could convince them was by removing his watch. He always left his watch on when he sunbathed and when he took his watch off, there was this absolutely brilliant white watch mark on his arm. That was what convinced the local Arabs that he was still one of us.

When I first went out to Tunisia, I was given one hotel to look after and it had never had English tourists before. The tourists in the past had been Germans and the German system was that there was one courier looking after five or six hotels, so consequently he or she was never in one hotel for any length of time. If the customers had complaints they had to wait until the next time they saw their rep, and the Arabs had got used to this method of not being bothered very much. When I moved into the hotel in Sousse, I was resident in the hotel with my clients, so when there was a complaint I would go and deal with it immediately and in the strange local mentality they decided that it was because of me that they were getting all these complaints. They did not realise it was because of the system, so they also reasoned that if they got rid of me they would get rid of the complaints. Now one thing that you are up against when you are working in an environment like that is that everyone is related to everyone else. So for a start, you are an alien in more than one sense, and being a woman you are definitely a second class citizen. I had a very short time to adjust and find out what was to be done to preserve my sanity and keep my holiday-makers happy.

One of the incidents that I remember very vividly was the business with the coach driver and the suitcases. In Tunisia the individual coaches that ferried the passengers to and from the airport were usually owned by the hoteliers themselves and so Mohammed's brother, Mohammed, would drive the coach. But when I was taking a party of tourists back to the airport to say goodbye to them after a fortnight's holiday, the Arab coach driver did not understand that if the tourists tipped me it was for the two weeks' service they just had. He considered that the tip was for the coach ride and was very upset when he didn't get his share.

No one had explained this to me, so I wasn't ready for what happened after the first three or four groups of holiday-makers had set off reasonably happily back to London. I was arranging for a transfer of a coach load of people back to the airport. As normal, I had told everyone to assemble at 7a.m. and to line up their suitcases outside the hotel's main entrance so that we could load the luggage on the coach. This was done and the traditional returning home luggage was all laid out – suitcases bulging at the seams, the inevitable ten or so large bird cages. I always hoped that people bought the ornamental bird cages that the Tunisians sold to put plants in, because as bird cages they were absolutely abysmal. For a start, they were painted with lead paint and the shape copied the pattern of the dome on the mosque, as most things do in the Arab countries. That was fine for a mosque dome but a long upright base part and then a balloon at the top was useless as far as the birds were concerned. It meant that the birds had to fly like helicopters and go straight up before they could fly around, and I just cannot think of any bird whose flight mimics a helicopter. So all these precious souvenirs and suitcases bulging with heaven knows what, the illicit duty frees or whatever, were lined up outside the hotel waiting to be loaded. The coach driver was deter-mined that this was the morning that he was going to make me see the light and persuade me that I should be coughing up some of the readies his way. When he pulled into the semi-circle in front of the hotel, instead of parking as he would normally for the luggage to be loaded, he drove right round the semi-circle and straight over a line of thirty-five suitcases. They were crushed completely, the bird cages were mangled in all directions and then the driver just drove away. I ran into the manager of the hotel and screamed at the top of my voice that the coach had just driven over all the suitcases and that if he looked out of his window he could see them. He denied the whole thing. Not only did he deny it but the receptionist denied it, the head waiter denied it, the gardener denied it, I should imagine anyone within a five-mile radius of the hotel would swear blind on a stack of Korans that the coach and driver had never been anywhere near the suitcases. This was his way of letting me know that he did not feel that he was getting his share. It was a nightmare for me to fill out all the insurance claim forms and pacify these demented tourists. It did not work, though, he still did not get any money.

From then on, whenever I was taking a party of people back to the airport on the coach, I would tell them all the traditional things about having their passports ready and their tickets and making sure that they had not left anything behind. Then I would say very rapidly in quite a broad north-eastern accent, so that even if by some remote chance the Arab spoke good English he certainly would not catch what I was saying, that 'this cretin who is sat here driving the bus' (then I would point to him and smile and they would all laugh and he would think that I was introducing him to them) 'is a greedy pig and if you in your generosity have decided that you would like to give me a tip, then please do so when we are out of vision of this greedy sod here, because otherwise he expects half of it when he has done sod all to get it' and everybody would laugh and I would say, 'Give him a round of applause' and they would all give him a round of applause and be hysterical and he would smile and wave back. That way I got round the tipping problem.

But the hotel staff were determined to get rid of me. They made my life an absolute misery. All the holiday representa-tives were given accommodation in hotels that couldn't poss-ibly be sold to any paying customer – in other words it was really the worst end of the deal. We were living in rooms in an annexe at the bottom of the garden and my room was so damp that within a couple of days any leather shoes I owned were green with mould, I used to have to dry my bed out every night with my hair dryer before I could get into it, but the job was so exhausting that I managed to sleep anyway. They would wait until I was absolutely sound asleep and then come right outside my bedroom window and start to play the traditional Tunisian musical instruments which, to put it mildly, sounded like a cat being castrated without an anaesthetic. When they were absolutely sure that I was wide awake, they would go away.

Another thing that really upset me was that they would send all my letters from England back with 'Not known at this address' written on it and my mother was going frantic thinking I had been whisked off by the white slave trade. One day I was told that there was a parcel in the reception of the hotel for me and I thought, 'Oh, thank God for that, somebody has remembered that I exist' because I was getting really worried: I had had no mail and no contact with the outside world at all. When I went up to reception they were all standing round and there was this box on the reception desk. I opened it straight away, not realising that this was their idea of a joke and also their way of telling me that I should leave, because when I opened the box there was a huge lizard inside and it was alive. They had caught it in the garden. Of course, because I am so interested in all living creatures, I was just fascinated by it and I didn't know what it was. I figured that if they had put it in the box it couldn't have been poisonous, so I picked it out of the box, examined it carefully and then took it out and released it into the garden. That was my big mistake: I had made absolutely sure that the perpetrators of the warning and so-called joke had totally lost face and above all else they would not stand for that. Word got back to my boss, who was based in Tunis, that I must leave the hotel that day or I would leave but I wouldn't be standing up. So they moved me immediately into another hotel that had had English tourists for quite some time.

It was a very big hotel: we had 350 guests in there and I shared looking after them with another courier from the same company. He was an Arab, a Moroccan, and through him I learnt much more quickly how to deal with the quirks and mentality of the locals and survived to make money and quite often to have a lot of fun. He was the traditional holiday courier with a different woman every week and I could never understand what the girls saw in him because he was grossly unattractive, but he had all the patter that goes with the job and he was reasonably well educated. Some of the gullible girls that would fall into his clutches used to drive me crackers. I would try and warn them but they would never listen to me. He actually had a card index of all the women he conquered throughout the season with their names and addresses and a few notes about them so that when they wrote to him he could write back the appropriate reply and then he would use all these addresses and he lived for nothing all through the winter going and visiting all these dumb women. Incredible. I can't imagine all the diseases he must have picked up and passed on in his time but he was having a great time.

Fortunately for me, Malcolm has always been keen on animals as well but there are a few things that he still cannot cope with and in Tunisia there was one graphic example. We had a very poky room with a shower and a tiny sink. At certain times of the year the huge cockroaches used to take flight: no one had warned us about this and we got back to the room one day to find half a dozen of these things joyfully playing along the head of the bed. Normally we would just sweep them out of the room into the garden with a brush and close the door. On this day, when Malcolm got the brush and swept them off the bed head, they took flight and it was as though we were being dive-bombed. Both of us screamed, it was such a shock, and we hit the deck while these things went buzzing around the room. The other weapon we used to attack these giants of the insect world was a strange thing that I have never actually seen anywhere else. It was the Arab's version of a squeegee mop and it consisted of a broom handle with a rounded piece of wood on the end. It looked to all intents and purposes like a croquet mallet. The Arab ladies would put a cloth in a bucket of water, hook it out with the croquet mallet, swing it round to drain off some of the water and then push the cloth with the croquet mallet along the floor: it really worked quite efficiently. So I had what we called a 'stick and cloth' in the corner of my bathroom for the maid to swab out the bathroom. We used to use this mallet as a weapon to get rid of unwanted room guests, such as when these cockroaches started to fly and all landed on the ceiling. Croquet and polo were nothing compared to Malcolm jumping up and down

126

on the bed with his wooden thing trying to knock the cock-roaches off the ceiling and jumping out of the way as soon as they moved again so that they wouldn't touch him.

The most extraordinary member of the insect family that ever tried to share our accommodation was the biggest moth I have ever seen. One day when we came home, I went straight into the bathroom, used the loo, came out and did not notice anything. Malcolm went into the bathroom, got halfway through using the loo, shouted and obviously turned very quickly. He managed to spray his shoes and halfway up the bathroom wall and run out into the bedroom not quite decent to tell me to go and have a look in the sink. It was the biggest 'bloody moth' he had ever seen. I went in and there was this enormous creature with its proboscis down the plug hole trying to drink. It really was a monster. The span of its wings was as big as my hand and the only way I could catch it was to wrap my hand in my very precious toilet paper: having soft toilet paper in Tunisia in those days was sort of the equivalent to having a mink-lined toilet seat in this country. You paid a pound a roll for this soft toilet paper and when I was only earning twelve pounds a week, you can imagine how much of a luxury that was. So it was used very Spartanly, two squares at a time, and when you suffered from dysentery as often as I did, it could be quite an expensive process. I wrapped my precious toilet paper round my hand and actually picked up this moth and took it outside and it was a handful. It was quite an extraordinary feeling holding an insect that big. Every day after that, Malcolm would send me into the bathroom first, just to make sure. We always had to remember to fill a bucket of water up and put it over the plug hole because the system of 'U' bends that we have in this country and take absolutely for granted did not seem to figure in the plumbing pattern of North Africa, so you could get all sorts of amazing things crawling up your plug hole to meet you. But it was fun.

One of the funniest things was when one of my tourists broke his fingers diving into the swimming pool. Okay, it wasn't funny for him at the time, but I remember taking him up to the hospital and going into the waiting room. If you had an injury, you had to take off all your dressings before you went into the doctor's surgery and with their usual standards of hygiene and cleanliness, the Tunisians would just drop all these blood-soaked dressings on the floor in the waiting room. It did not seem that anyone ever swept them up – the whole place was an absolutely stinking mass of blood-soaked bandages, orange peel and all sorts of other debris. It was also full of tribal, nomadic, bedouin-type people who were probably on their once-a-year visit into town and took advantage of the opportunity to have all their illnesses seen to at the same time as they did their shopping. I was always under the impression that you caught more than you actually got put right if you stood around very long in this kind of environment.

The tourist was in quite a lot of pain, he had really jarred his fingers quite badly and we were told that he had to go for an X-ray. As I mentioned before, the key to earning a living as a courier is to get commission on everything you get your holidaymakers to do. If they buy souvenirs from a certain shop you get commission. If they get their photographs developed at a certain place, you get commission. If you recommend them to a restaurant, you get commission, etc., etc. But what was about to happen was certainly a first for me. We went into the radiology department in the hospital, which in itself was a sight for sore eyes. I have always thought that there should be a great deal of personal security involved in radiology as the X-rays themselves are quite dangerous if you are over-exposed, but the radiologist did not seem to be too bothered. In fact, he had a cigarette hanging out of his mouth and as he laid the client out on the table, stretched the chap's hand out and spread his fingers (much to the guy's dismay and agony), the cigarette ash from the drooping cigarette fell on to the patient's arm. The radiologist just blew it off with the delightful breath people have when they haven't cleaned their teeth for several years and took a couple of X-rays. He then said that the chap had to wait outside, which he did. He came back and asked if I was interested in making the usual arrangements as he had never met me before. By this time, I was pretty much aware that most people were in most things for money and I wondered how much he expected me to pay him for the client's X-rays. But it didn't take me long to find out that he was into making a deal with me for the actual X-ray plates: apparently a number of the other couriers whose holiday-makers had had accidents bought the X-ray plates from him and sold them to their holiday-makers at a substantial profit as a unique holiday souvenir. There is one thing that you really have to admire the Arabs for – they never miss a trick when it comes to making an extra dinar or two.

My working life in Tunisia came to an abrupt halt. I had not been feeling well for some time and I began to lose weight rapidly: even though I was eating every twenty minutes I would often collapse. I returned to England weighing seven stone, and as I am five foot six I didn't look particularly wonderful. After seeing a doctor I was admitted to the Royal Victoria Infirmary in Newcastle. During my stay I noticed an article in the regional newspaper saying that a franchise had been granted to open an independent local radio station in Stockton-on-Tees. I wrote at once to the proposed managing director, saying that unless he found a place for me the station was bound to be a failure. I waited for a reply for ages, during which time I underwent loads of tests. Finally they agreed they didn't know what was wrong with me! I was getting better without treatment, and I was discharged. I still suffer now and then with a milder form of the symptoms, but nothing to worry about.

When my answer finally came from the radio station, it was by telephone. The newly appointed programme controller rang and interviewed me for an hour over the phone. I was offered a job then and there. I don't suppose your appearance is so critical for radio, only what you sound like. I was told later that my letter had been the sole occupant of a filing cabinet for several weeks.

October

I don't like October. It's neither one thing nor the other. All the leaves are falling from the trees and it always seems such a bleak time of year. We get the fierce winds from the west which make my ears ache and spook all the animals, but at least it is not so busy on the animal front. We'll have no more orphaned youngsters until next year and Malcolm should be able to keep a pair of socks intact for a while. Have you ever noticed when you go to the launderette that you often come back and empty your washing to find one sock missing? In the Willis household, even after we bought a washing machine, Malcolm still found he had only one sock from each pair of his favourites. Let me explain. Socks are ideal for holding injured birds in position while their wings set. A nice stretchy nylon sock with a hole cut out of the toe can snugly fit most birds from pigeon size to owls and even kestrels. At this time of year, migrating birds have sensibly disappeared from our shores to seek sunnier climates. I miss the calls of the curlews. We have regular visitors each year who come to nest in an adjacent field to the cottage. It always makes me feel good when I hear the haunting cries of the parent birds reclaiming their territory. Curlews are ground-nesting birds and it is not easy to find their chosen nesting site. They will always land a long way from it and make their way through the long grass on foot. One day, I was out in the fields exercising Suzi, my tiny crossbreed, and it was through the sensitivity of her nose that I had the pleasure of seeing the curlew young still in the nest. I often go out with Suzi and leave Rags and Baxter at home. They are far too boisterous and warn wildlife for miles around that we are coming. With Suzi, it's different – she is gentle and sensitive with absolutely no killer instinct. When she finds something interesting, she quietly lets me know, running backwards and forwards until I approach her new-found treasure. On this particular day, she was very excited and led me through the long grass which was soon to be hay and there I found, perfectly concealed to the human eye, two curlew chicks.

We watched them for quite some time and I was furious that I didn't have my camera. The parent birds became more and more agitated and were buzzing us like a pair of wartime

Spitfires – dive-bombing ever nearer – so we soon left them in peace and as I left I hoped the young would be back next year. Suzi is without doubt the animal I love most in the whole world. We have always had a very special relationship. She is a very old lady now at fifteen, but still full of fun and capable of acting just like a puppy. When she was very young and we were staying with friends, Keith used to tickle her tummy with his toes, which she loved. It does not take long for animals to catch on to something they like. To this day, if you sit with your legs stretched out and your feet crossed at the ankles, she will take this as a personal invitation. It has caused a few embarrassing moments as she has walked over to someone who is not in the know and cocked her leg up over their feet. Most people, not realising what she is doing, and also not remembering that she is a bitch, think they are about to have their shoes anointed with pee. Many a cup of coffee has ended up in someone's lap as they have moved quickly to dodge the oncoming flow.

Suzi is so special she was my bridesmaid at my wedding. She had a beautiful pale blue satin bow and the Registrar was not amused. In fact, halfway through the proceedings, he stopped because I was giggling and reminded us of the solemnity of the occasion. Some people have no sense of humour. When Suzi was young, her constant companion was a black rabbit. They would play for hours and even slept together. Eventually the partnership had to come to an end – the rabbit turned out to be a buck and became extremely aggressive. We didn't need 'Beware of the Dog' signs on our gate but who would have believed 'Beware of the Rabbit'? He started to attack everyone, including Suzi. I think he had amorous designs towards her. There was only one solution – castration. Aren't men sensitive about this subject? I had to take him to the vet, Malcolm couldn't even bring himself to discuss it. The deadly deed was done but it didn't seem to do much good. He lived to a ripe old age and he did lose some of his spark but then, wouldn't we all? At least he was a bit safer to have around.

It was around this time of year that I was very busy when I worked for the record company. My job was labelled 'promotions representative': this meant that I was working

132

from home but doing a lot of travelling to radio and television stations and the main record shops. As I mentioned previously, I always used these opportunities to seek out pet shops, but I also made a lot of good contacts in zoos up and down the country. Whenever I visited Edinburgh I used to make a habit of staying in the Post House Hotel, not exactly five-star but for me it surpassed all of the other hotels in Edinburgh because it overlooked the zoo. After numerous visits, I became very friendly with many of the keepers there and particularly the ones in the reptile house. My job meant that I had to pay regular visits to London and it didn't take long for the people in Edinburgh to realise what a valuable courier they had in me. On one occasion, a particularly enthusiastic young keeper in Edinburgh had set up a culture of wax moths. Keepers of reptiles in captivity have problems related not only to temperature and environment but mainly to feeding their charges. Many reptiles will not accept anything other than live food. The traditional use of meal-worms is not sufficient as a balanced diet. Mealworms are only as good as the food they are fed on. Consequently, there has always been a search for more nourishing yet easily available food. To this end, Edwin, the keeper, had been experimenting on breeding wax moths, the larvae of which are much more nourishing than mealworms. Mr David Ball, the curator of reptiles at Regent's Park Zoo, was very keen to obtain such a culture. I was more than happy to assist and carry the unusual cargo on my next visit to London.

Unfortunately, London traffic was particularly bad that day. I had no time to call into the zoo before going to my meeting. The restaurant where we had lunch was very hot and stuffy and the box under my chair started to make peculiar noises as the wax moth larvae became active. Have you ever tried to explain to your boss why you have got a box of what he thinks are maggots under your chair in one of the more up-market London restaurants?

It was through Edinburgh Zoo that I was given one of the tortoises that I still own today. I have had her for nine years now. Any zoo or animal collection will tell you that people arrive regularly with unwanted pets that they think they can simply dump into the care of the keepers and go away with a clear conscience. Of course, this is totally impractical – it's particularly bad with terrapins, which grow much bigger than most people realise, and in years gone by, before the ban on the import of tortoises in January 1984 (after which they became very valuable), people did not think twice about leaving them in reptile collections up and down the country.

This particular tortoise was a very small female spur-thighed. She had a tiny head and an abscess almost as big as her head coming out from what would be the tortoise's ear. At that time, Edinburgh Zoo did not feel that they could take on this sick animal as the overworked staff could not give it the individual attention it would obviously require, so they offered it to me and as always I was a 'softie' – I can never say no. The abscess was so big in relation to the size of the tortoise that her mouth was becoming deformed and she was unable to bite through anything harder than a banana. I sought the help of one of the most marvellous men I have ever met, Dr Oliphant Jackson. He is one of life's characters, a highly qualified veterinary surgeon and a rarity in as much as he specialises in reptiles. As I have said before, people with an enthusiasm for their chosen role in life are ageless. Dr Jackson retired a few years ago and I am sure he has worked harder than ever since then. His enthusiasm is contagious. He talks with love about his favourite animals and his lectures are renowned throughout the herpetological world. He willingly operated on the unfortunate animal which was by now christened 'Number 3'. (When you have as many animals as I do, you run out of names.) The operation left the tortoise with a gaping hole in her head and left me with a lot of patient after-care. Because of the deformity of her mouth, she found it extremely difficult to eat, so every day I made purées of banana, strawberry, apple and whatever other tempting morsels I could persuade her to eat. With regular bathing, the wound healed and using an emery board, I slowly reshaped the misshapen beak-like mouth. She is now a large healthy lady who I hope will produce some eggs in the not too distant future. As I write this now she is ready to go into hibernation but will be held back for another few weeks in artificial heat to duplicate her natural environment. Because our winter is so long, tortoises cannot eat enough in the summer months to last them through the winter. If we just left them to sleep until the weather was warmer, they would die of starvation.

Hibernation does not only affect creatures of the more temperate climates but we have a fair share of winter sleepers in the British Isles. Hedgehogs spend the summer eating virtually continuously to lay down the stores of fat they will need to see them through the long sleep. I get many letters from people telling me about their regular night-time visitor, covered in spines and equally endowed with fleas. Fleas are one of the few creatures that I would choose not to have a close encounter with if at all possible. One mild October's evening when I was taking the dogs for their last walk, Rags encountered his first hedgehog. Rags is not a particularly bright dog, in fact the phrase 'The lights are on but there's no one at home' describes him perfectly. Rags will catch anything that moves and is mouth-size, including hedge-hogs. Even after that first encounter, he has never learnt to leave them alone; despite suffering a lacerated mouth and an infestation of more than willing fleas, he will still repeat the process at any given opportunity. It is not easy to rescue a hedgehog.

If you are ever in a position where you need to rescue a hedgehog, direct contact is not recommended. Apart from the obvious problem of the spines, the hedgehog's parasites can so easily become yours. This is particularly important to remember if you are unfortunate enough to be dealing with a dying animal. Most parasites are attracted to their host's body warmth, so a dying creature will not be a very inviting place to live and your warm-blooded proximity will soon seem infinitely preferable. If your hedgehog has received a minor injury, then the best treatment is just to leave it in a warm, dark place to recuperate for a few hours. If there are any obvious wounds which are within easy access, then treatment with veterinary powder is one of the best I can recommend. This powder can be bought in soft polythene bottles and a sharp squeeze will propel the powder into the wound and even reach between the hedgehog's spines. If you are not within easy reach of a cardboard box in which to roll your hedgehog, the best course of action is to wrap it in something disposable and carry it back home hammock fashion. Stress is often a major factor in the death of wild animals and so minimum handling is the best course for you and for the hedgehog.

Rags still persists in his attacks on the local hedgehogs but I think that they must be getting wise to him, as he now rarely succeeds in doing any damage. Fortunately these days Rags's vicious tendencies are directed towards those members of the animal kingdom that are not part of the Willis household. In years gone by this was not the case: not only did he attempt to kill every animal in the vicinity but also every other human apart from Malcolm and myself. I first found Rags one winter's morning in deep snow in the garden of the flat which we had in Norton. At first, I didn't notice him at all, he was huddled in a corner and partially covered in snow. He was too weak to stand and appeared to have been in that position for most of the night. I carried him into the flat. He was drastically underweight for his size, and when I first saw him, he resembled a pile of old cleaning clothes poured into a small heap on the ground, hence the name Rags.

His coat was matted and soaked, he had mucus running from his eyes and could hardly find the strength to lap a saucer of warm milk. I dried him off as much as I could and allowed him to sleep in front of the gas fire while he regained his strength. Three hours later, he took a small portion of solid food – it is never wise to overfeed a starving animal, as its undernourished system cannot cope and either vomiting or severe diarrhoea will be the result. That after-noon, I took him to the vet who was very pessimistic about his chances of survival. However, I persuaded him that I was willing to try and so, I started the long-term mercy treatment that resulted in the large sturdy animal that I own today, fifteen years later. On close examination, we found that his hair had grown into huge matted balls virtually obstructing his ear passages. His underside was covered in a severe rash and he was a fifth of the weight that he should have been for a dog his size. He appeared to be an Airedale crossbreed, the overall colour being dark grey. It took more than a week to clip away the matted coat carefully and gently clean his skin which was very sore, probably due to the fact that he had obviously lived rough for sometime. It only took him three days to realise that he had found a good home and however weakly to set about the task of defending it. No one apart from Malcolm and myself was allowed to enter the flat and as soon as he gained enough strength to make it to the garden, that was his domain as well. Once we got rid of his infection, he rapidly put on weight and the vet thought that he was somewhere in the region of two years old. It is always a problem taking on a dog that is fully grown. It is relatively easy with patience and kindness to train a puppy to your lifestyle, but an adult dog, especially one like Rags who had not been used to domesticity, was altogether another problem. He never caused the usual problems associated with puppies such as peeing on the carpet, but he did have some strange habits – one thing that he did which was particularly infuriating was to remove all the inner soles from any shoes he could find – and the worst problem of all was his viciousness. His fervent desire to protect the flat nearly resulted in his early demise. At this flat, we had regular visits from one of the local policemen who was a keen bird fancier. As is often the case, when members of the public do not know what to do, they contact the police, particularly when they have found a stray or injured animal. Birds of all shapes and sizes were often found and delivered to the local station. This particular caring policeman would take time out to bring them to us in the hope that we could get them back to health. Apart from being a regular policeman, he had done a long spell of duty as a dog handler. On this particular day, not long after Rags had shown his intention of protecting us from the whole world, our friendly policeman arrived for a visit. I was in the garden with Rags, who was by now quite strong, when our friend's head appeared over the garden gate. He had not been to the flat for a while so he had yet to encounter Rags. He was just about to come through the gate when I spotted him and shouted at him to wait. Rags was on guard immediately. I explained it would be best for him to wait outside until I locked Rags in the flat. He wouldn't hear of it.

'Don't worry about me, I'm used to dogs, I've worked with them for years!'

With this, he opened the gate. Rags took a flying leap and latched on to the bottom part of his jacket. I lunged for Rags but before I could pull him away he had a mouthful of uniform.

'Oh, bloody hell, the sergeant will kill me.'

He couldn't do much about it, as I had warned him, and actually he turned out to be very understanding. It was midway through my profuse apologies that I remembered I had forgotten to buy a dog licence! Fortunately, he was too shaken to think about anything as mundane as that. We did not see him for quite some time and the next time he called, he telephoned first saying he was on his way.

However much I tried I could not make Rags understand that other people should be allowed to visit the flat. It created dreadful problems and soon sorted out are true and understanding friends from the casual acquaintance variety. The normal pattern for an evening's entertainment would be to lock Rags in the bedroom and watch the horror on your guests' faces as the snarling maniac gave vent to his aggression on the bedroom door. On one occasion, when it was time for Rags's evening walk, Malcolm went into the bedroom and put him on his lead. He then had to drag him through the living room past our quaking friends and take him downstairs, snarling and dripping saliva all the way. I happened to be standing between the guests and the dog and as he lurched forward to tear out their throats, his jaws closed round the top of my leg and I was quite badly bitten. It was obvious to me that he did not intend to bite me but I could not allow this sort of thing to go unpunished. I immediately took the dog from Malcolm and shook him like a rag – I would never be able to do that now as he weighs far too much. He was very shocked at being on the receiving end of the first punishment he'd ever had from me. But it was important for me to gain superiority over him there and then as the dog is basically a pack animal and must never forget who the leader is. Shaking him by the scruff of the neck is the way he would have been disciplined by his mother and is therefore, I feel, the most effective treatment. He has never attempted anything like that again.

Two regular visitors, Stuart and Barbara, were also great animal lovers but even they were petrified at the sight of the demented Rags. However, it was Stuart who eventually turned the tide and made it possible for all our future visitors to sit in peace. One particular night we had had dinner along with copious quantities of wine. At this stage, we were bringing Rags into the room as he was always kept on the lead. He would sit reasonably quietly until either Stuart or Barbara made a move, even if it was just to pick up a glass, but when they did he would lurch forward in their direction and growl and bare his teeth. It didn't make for the most pleasant of evenings, however fond they were of animals. It certainly tried our guests' patience and also radically cut down our drinks bill. Despite the growling, or even because of it, Stuart did manage to get very drunk. As we all know, drunks are not famed for their wisdom and suddenly Stuart in a defiant-verging-on-the-insane burst of courage decided that enough was enough. A mixture of whisky and dry white wine fuelled his fervour and he did the unthinkable. He stood up. Not only did he stand up but he walked determinedly across the room and towards Rags. I had only been feeling slightly tipsy but was immediately stone cold sober at the prospect of seeing my old friend torn limb from limb. Rags was taken totally by surprise – without a pause, Stuart walked straight up to him and said in a most sober-like voice, 'Shut up and sit down.' Rags stopped in mid-growl and obeyed. This was what he needed – somebody who was not traditionally part of our pack with the courage to stand up to him. Several whiskies later, Stuart's bravado increased to the point where he was actually stroking the dog. I remember the following day Stuart phoning with a dreadful hangover and asking me to confirm his wife's story that he had actually stood up to Rags and lived to tell the tale without any obvious wounds other than a stinking headache. He was justly proud of this feat and subsequently dined out on the story at many of our less brave friends' houses.

It was not long after this tide-turning event that we bought our first house. The day came when we were to move and the furniture van arrived. Rags was confined to the kitchen while we loaded the furniture on to the van. He was extremely distressed but we put this down to the fact that he was not keen on strangers constantly moving up and down the stairs. However, mid-morning, we finally discovered the story of Rags's tragic beginning. He escaped from the kitchen and fled downstairs, through the open door into the garden and straight out through the back gate. I was terrified that he would attack the removal men – after all they did appear to be stealing our things. I made chase down the stairs expecting to find a scene of bloody carnage, but I could not see Rags anywhere. As I ran through the back gate and passed the furniture van, out of the corner of my eye I thought I saw movement. On closer inspection, I discovered Rags. He was sitting in the very top left hand corner of the back of the van on top of our piled up furniture, shaking like a leaf.

His sad history then fell into place. It was obvious to me that sometime in his past his original owners had also moved house, with one exception – they had not included Rags. That would explain the emaciated state in which I found him and his obvious terror at the events that were taking place. Once the move was finally over and we were all together in the new house, he became a different animal, finally realising that he had a home for life – whether it be this house or the flat he would always be with us. He still has the ability to sound like a ferocious monster and I am sure if need be he could still defend me or my property, but all in all he has turned out to be a big softie.

When we eventually moved to the cottage, we discovered that, however nice his nature had become, he was still a danger to wildlife and an even bigger danger to sheep. He still can't be allowed off the lead when we go for a walk in the country. When you live in a farming community, one of the biggest sins is to own a sheep-worrying dog. If he was caught in the act, my neighbours would not hesitate to shoot him and I would expect them to do so. It is the responsibility of all of us to keep our animals under control wherever they are.

One of the things that Rags loves most of all is water. I

have never known a dog to enjoy a bath so much. He will often attempt to climb in the bath with either Malcolm or myself if he is given half a chance. The cry of 'bath time' results in Rags dashing to the bathroom in eager anticipation and Suzi cowering under the bed as though she was about to be drowned. Whenever we take the dogs to the river, whatever time of the year it may be, Rags will plunge into the water and if it is only shallow he will lie down to make sure he gets well and truly soaked. Baxter, the puppy, hasn't taken long to copy his idol, Rags, and plunge with equal enthusiasm into the often icy flow. It's just as well, because he has grown a very long coat resembling an ill-kempt Afghan hound and regularly needs bathing.

Fortunately, Baxter has not developed Rags's dislike for sheep. We made sure of this by using an old country remedy. When he was still a very young and curious puppy, we took him on to a farm and introduced him to a small flock of old experienced ewes and their very domineering ram, or tupp, as he is known by the local name. Baxter was taught in no uncertain terms that dogs do not mess with sheep and get off lightly. After the second head butt from the tupp which sent him flying through the flock, he was smart enough to catch on. After this incident, we feel completely safe to allow him to run free on his daily walk. It was the same sort of remedy which taught him to live and let live with all the other animals that share his home. Once you have been bitten by a macaw, had your nose bitten by a ferret, been chased by a demented chicken and propelled down the garden by a goat, you rapidly learn to live at peace with your neighbours.

I have often been asked for advice from people who have owned a dog for a number of years and then decide to buy a puppy. They complain that fights are a problem and that often the older dog will be seen to bite the young one quite viciously. They then perpetuate the problem by constantly separating the dogs, even going so far as to keep them in separate rooms. This creates a tremendous strain in the household and has often been the cause of people getting rid of a new puppy because they cannot manage. What I try to explain is that the youngster must learn to fit in to the pecking order of the household. Obviously the older dog is in possession of the territory at the time of the new arrival; he or she must be allowed to prove his dominance over the puppy and the puppy must show the signals that he accepts this for peace to reign. If you separate the fighting pair, you do not allow the whole system of dog language to run its course. Each time the fight is stopped without full submission being shown by the puppy, the whole affair will start again the next time they are reintroduced. I know it is hard to stand by and watch a young puppy apparently being 'savaged' by a much older dog. But unless you allow this to play out its full course, the problems will constantly re-occur. It is just the same when introducing any new animal or bird into an established collection. There are occasions when an older creature will not accept a new arrival at any price, and then obviously we must interfere, but generally if the new arrival is not a mature adult the introduction should go relatively smoothly after the initial confrontation.

November

The long dark nights are here and animal management becomes more and more difficult. The shorter days mean less feeding time for the birds and less time to do everything in for the humans. The garden gets soaked and the once lush grass turns to a mud heap. The goats spend more and more time indoors and the electricity bills go up as all the more tropical animals are brought indoors under artificial heat. Fruit and vegetables rocket in price and the food bills soar. All this and I've got to think about buying Christmas presents as well! I have always harboured a secret wish to be able to disappear at the start of the Christmas mayhem and come back when it's all over. I have always thought Christmas is for children but most people, particularly my mother, cannot understand my desire to miss out on the whole affair. Commercial pressure dictates that Christmas cards and presents must be bought in plenty of time, including gifts for the respective dogs and cats. I always forget to hide everything and usually come home one day in mid-November to find the floor covered with the remnants of the boxes of Doggie Chocolate Drops and Kitty Treats that the animals have discovered and helped themselves to.

It has never been a particularly tidy house for obvious reasons and one little creature gave us quite a bit of additional mess for a short while – a tiny golden coloured bantam hen. She was a great character. She came to me because she was the smallest and last in line in the pecking order of our neighbour's son David's collection. When she arrived, she was in a very bad way – she'd lost most of her tail feathers and was bleeding badly around her face and beak. Because she needed individual attention, she became extremely tame and lived in her own little hen hut in the side garden away from the larger and more boisterous hens. Her particular little house was situated not far from the small kitchen window that the cats use to get in and out. It didn't take her long to cotton on to what was going on and capitalise on the situation. One day we came home to the cottage and found her in the kitchen. The next day we came home and found her in the living room having left several parcels of black and white hen droppings on route. The day after I came home and did not notice she was in the house. After my usual animal check, I discovered that she was missing and feared the worst. It was a particularly cold afternoon and I searched the immediate vicinity for signs of a recent fox kill. I did not find anything and went back indoors to make some coffee which I took to my usual chair in the living room. My favourite comfie seat is opposite the television and there just below the set and squeezed into a small gap I spotted little hen sitting on the video. Obviously it was a toasty place and she was seeking out the warmth. This became quite a regular occurrence and I was constantly taking her back into the garden to try and educate her about rightful hen behaviour.

It was not long after this that I came home one day and found her in the house in obvious distress. The treatment for distressed birds is peace and quiet and a great deal of heat. She was obviously searching for this but I had arrived home too late and she died not long afterwards. On post-mortem I discovered that she was badly egg-bound. This can often happen with all sorts of birds in periods of sudden cold weather. If I had got to her in time, the normal treatment would have been to rub a little oil around her vent and confine her in a hospital cage at a temperature of around 90°F. If that did not work, the final remedy would have been to hold the bird over a steaming kettle. The steam acts on the bird the way it acts on humans in a Turkish bath, opening pores and generally relaxing muscles. I stress that this is the final treatment as it can often cause a great deal of stress to an already unwell bird, particularly if they are not used to being handled.

I said earlier that the stories of birds and the Willises are legion. It was at this time of year that I was recuperating from a very serious attack of pleurisy. I had awoken one morning with quite a bad earache, and as I was not a person who suffered with ear problems, I took a couple of pain killers and went back to bed to try to sleep it off. It persisted and got worse and in the end I was in absolute agony. It felt as if someone was poking a huge knitting needle into my ear and I was crying with the pain. I really felt like bouncing my head off the wall. It lasted all day and by the middle of that evening I could stand it no longer. I telephoned the doctor whose wife answered but Malcolm had to continue the call for me. She could hear me screaming in the background and her husband came straight round. He gave me an injection of antibiotics and some sleeping tablets and said I should feel better in the next couple of days. I did not. My head began to swell, my eyes closed and the whole viral infection began to take over my respiratory system. I began to look like the elephant man and the pain unbelievably got worse. When the doctor came again, he was extremely worried as by now I had very obvious difficulty in breathing. It was agony – I was taking short sharp gasps and had not even got the energy to sit upright. I had never been in such a dreadful state. The doctor took some tests and said he was very concerned because he thought I had contracted psittacosis. This is a disease which is carried by birds and is one of the reasons we have our quarantine laws. Imported birds are kept in strict quarantine conditions and tested for several diseases including psittacosis. I have always taken great precautions when dealing with birds, and particularly in the dry summer time when there is a lot of dust around, I always wear a surgeon's disposable face-mask when I am cleaning out the aviary. Despite the fact that I owned no recently imported birds, the doctor felt that this was an obvious diagnosis as I spent so much time with my collection.

Finally, the tests came back and it may sound ridiculous now but I was happy to find that I actually had pleurisy. Despite the fact that I was very ill, I was relieved to know that there was no reason why I must get rid of my birds. Pleurisy is one of the worst things that I have ever experienced and I would not wish it on my worst enemy. It was agony to breathe and I could not do anything. I was incapable of any kind of exertion, and was more or less immobilised. I remember one occasion when I could not stop myself from sneezing and it felt as if my chest cavity would burst.

When I was eventually recuperating, we went out for a drive in the country and despite the chill November air, it was a joy to take deep breaths and stroll around outdoors. All the swelling had disappeared but I had no idea how much the whole thing had taken out of my system. After my short walk, we were driving home and in a field in the distance I spotted a rook that was walking along dragging its wing. We stopped the car – it was obvious the bird needed help. If it could not fly, it would not have a chance of survival in the wild. It was in the middle of a large ploughed field where the earth had been turned into great huge furrows to allow the winter's frosts to do their work of breaking up the soil in readiness for the next season's crop. Malcolm ran to the far end of the field and chased the rook back towards me. As usual at times like these, concern for my own safety and common sense were not uppermost in my mind. I ran as fast as I could and eventually threw my coat over the rook and caught it. By the time Malcolm reached me from the far end of the field, I was in a dreadful state. I had totally over-exerted myself and was back to being a quivering wreck, sitting in the mud holding a bundle of coat and rook and hardly able to breathe at all.

Malcolm had to carry me, the coat and the rook back to the car and drive us home. It took me two or three days to get over it but apart from an injured wing the rook was fine. It had a severely dislocated wing but otherwise was a magnificent bird. If you have only seen a rook at a distance, you might think it is a fairly uninteresting black bird. At close quarters, rooks are quite different. Their shiny feathers shimmer with purple and greenish light under the sun's rays. With their beautifully large beaks and inquisitive eyes, they are quite splendid. Rooks are the ones that look as if they are wearing trousers and are always to be found in large groups. The common crow you will see as part of a pair but a massive gathering or what is sometimes known as a parliament of rooks is quite impressive. All members of the crow family are easy to please in captivity as they will eat almost anything.

The wing injury proved to be impossible to repair and a couple of years later another rook in similar condition came to join the otherwise healthy, by now well-established member of the Willis household. Neither of them will ever be able to fly again but at least they have companionship and a territory of their own. Despite their lack of flying ability, they can bound about the aviary and with suitably placed perches can easily reach a height at which they feel safe. Apart from regular feeding, and a constant supply of fresh bathing water, the only other thing they need from me is an annual feather trim. As each rook has a dislocated wing which drags at floor level, it is essential that I cut back the long primary feathers each year as they regrow after a moult, otherwise the birds would get very dirty and be more susceptible to infection. Rooks are long-lived and extremely intelligent birds and particularly in the very early part of the year, there is a lot of interaction between our rooks and their wild, free-living counterparts. Apart from herons, rooks are our earliest nesting birds and pair up for life. Our two have not made any advances towards breeding but they certainly make a lot of noise at that time of year, late February or March. I have had them now for eight years – at one point, it looked as though they were going to live longer than me.

I feel very fortunate in that I have no inbuilt fear of animals. Each one is an individual to be treated with respect and understanding. We are not born with phobias, but acquire them as we acquire all our knowledge. In our most formative years we learn from our parents and it is at this time that we learn to fear the things that our parents fear. Adults who are frightened of spiders will always say 'My mother was terrified of them as well.' Fortunately, my father, with whom I shared most of my feelings for animals, had no fear of any living thing and when I first expressed an interest in snakes I was not discouraged in any way. In recent years, I have tried to do my best to educate people, and particularly the young, that snakes are not the slimy poisonous horrors that they are so often made out to be. Not long ago in the television studios, I had a very large boa constrictor which I was using on a programme. On that particular day, a couple had brought their twin three-year-old daughters to the studio to take part in a separate feature. Before the show I had the snake on the floor in the large reception area. It was used to being handled regularly and was as tame as you could expect an undomesticated animal to be. We had also taken the precaution of keeping it cool as snakes, like all reptiles, are cold-blooded animals and depend on external heat sources to get their systems working. While I was handling the snake, the two little three-year-olds spotted it. Like all children who have not been taught otherwise, they had a natural curiosity to find out more about this unknown animal. They were fascinated and I spent some time explaining to them how the snake moved without legs and how beautiful he was to touch. Both the children were happy to stroke the snake and were fascinated by his rippling body. They showed no fear whatsoever.

It was at this point that their mother and father reappeared on the scene. As soon as they saw what their children were doing, they both shouted warnings to them to be careful and keep away and immediately both children started to cry. In the space of five seconds, the wonder and magic that these children were sharing had changed to an irrational fear, instantly taught by their parents. That one incident will colour these children's judgement on all future reptile encounters. It made me feel very sad.

In the zoo, the reptile house is one of the busiest, invariably full of adults passing on inaccurate information to their children about the inhabitants. Fortunately, I never had that problem and when I came home from the pet shop with my first grass snake, the only pieces of advice I was given were the usual ones that I must take care of its needs myself and that I must make sure it was in a tank from which it could not escape.

When I was young I was always one of the smallest and weediest people in my class. My birthday is in August, so because of the way the school year was allocated, I was also one of the youngest. As with most people who communicate well with animals, I found it much more difficult to communicate with my fellow humans. I spent a lot of my childhood being frightened not only of school teachers but also of my classmates. This grass snake changed a lot of things. As most of my contemporaries had already learnt to fear snakes, for once I was in a superior position and I milked it for all it was worth. It was never more evident than when I visited the local recreation park. Pre snake-owning days, I would hover around the perimeter of the play-ground and watch all the bigger children playing on the swings. On the first occasion that I took my grass snake with me, I discovered just how powerful an ally it could be. Grass snakes when handled give off very powerful smells and this all helped to add to the myth that snakes were nasty. On that first afternoon when I got it out of my blazer pocket and put it down on the ground, the swings emptied in a second. Never one to miss an opportunity I soon began to use it on every occasion where I needed to overcome my nervousness with others. Heaven knows what the dry cleaners must have thought when my mother regularly took my blazer in in an attempt to get rid of the awful smell – 'awful', by the way, was my mother's description. I quite liked it, in fact I enjoy most animals' natural smells. There is nothing more appealing than the smell of a tiny puppy and nothing more appalling than the smell of a dirty human.

Snakes are the Houdinis of the animal world, they can squeeze out of the tiniest space which I found to my cost. On one occasion my grass snake disappeared for five weeks and I was sure that it had gone for ever. It eventually did make a reappearance, having somehow found its way into my father's tool-box in the shed.

I have only ever been bitten once by a snake but it was the most spectacular affair. I was recording an animal programme specifically aimed at educating people on the beauty of some of our less loved creatures. We were to include tarantulas, scorpions and snakes, I suppose three of the most hated members of the animal kingdom. To this end, I had borrowed these creatures from a zoo. The scorpion and tarantula bit went very well, they both behaved impeccably. Not so, when we came to the snake. I must stress at this point that it was entirely due to human error and not in any way the fault of the reptile. A young inexperienced keeper had been sent by the zoo to the studio. It was her first visit to a television studio and she was slightly overawed by the whole event. In fact she was so engrossed with what was happening around her she completely forgot about the snake. Normally, snakes are transported in large cotton bags like pillowcases with a string tied round the top. She had placed the snake's bag too near a heat vent and the poor animal became very distressed. As I mentioned previously, it is a wise move to keep reptiles cool if you intend to handle them. I was unaware of the snake's plight and when I opened the bag the snake did the only natural thing and attacked me. It was a very large boa constrictor, so obviously it was not venomous but had a very nasty bite. It struck out for my face and fortunately I lowered my head in time and it made contact with the top of my head, its lower fangs entering just above my hairline. Because it was so large and had such a big mouth, its upper fangs latched on to about halfway down the back of my head. I say fortunately as this is the one place on the human body with an extremely thin covering of flesh and therefore there was very little for the snake to lock on to. I have never seen studio staff move so quickly. All my would-be knights in shining armour disappeared in all directions and I was left to wrestle with my attacker alone. It was a relatively easy task to prise the snake off my head, but not quite so easy to get it back into the bag – it was not a happy animal. Eventually I did get it back with the help of the keeper but by this time blood was pouring down my face. As soon as the snake was safely confined, I was surrounded by eager offers of help. I went into the make-up department to get some first aid and I suppose partly because of shock and partly because of the speed of the attack, I was only aware of the wounds at the front, above my hairline. These were cleaned and dealt with and my make-up was repaired, ready for me to go back into the studio but just as I was about to leave the make-up artist stopped me as she spotted my blood-soaked collar. The puncture wounds from the back fangs were quite bad but for some reason, I could not feel them at all. I went back in and finished the programme without the snake. Our press officer at the time, never one to miss a good story, thought it would be ideal to release to the papers. I immediately vetoed this idea: for one thing I was supposed to be doing a bit of public relations work for snakes in general and for another thing I certainly did not want to offend my friends at the zoo by getting them bad publicity, as they had always been very helpful to me.

Three months after this incident, around the Christmas

holiday period – it's known as the silly season in newspapers, mainly due to the fact that the newspapers are filled
with more non-stories than usual, as very little is actually
happening – the story of my attack appeared in some of the
national dailies. I do not know how they got hold of it but
by the time it made print, it was totally inaccurate.
Suddenly, the snake was two feet longer, she was my own
pet, her name was Esmeralda and the story of the attack was
magnified beyond belief. Every word in the article was
inaccurate. My mother had a terrible fright when a neighbour
dashed round with a newspaper to tell her the bad news.
My mother, like most people, still believes what she reads
in the newspapers. I used to, but over the years I have
realised that just because it is in black and white it is not
necessarily true. At one time, over a space of two days, I
was pictured in every national newspaper and was
accredited with five different ages, four different addresses
and six different salaries – none of it was true. In a job such
as mine, it is sensible to ignore everything you read about
yourself. So many people like to believe the good bits and
then get very hurt by the bad publicity. After all, it is only
one person's opinion, and it is impossible to please
everyone. To put it in perspective, I always think what is in
the newspapers today is on the bottom of a parrot cage to-
morrow.

As soon as you get a job in the public eye, you are invited
to do all sorts of bizarre things. I have done my share of
declaring village fêtes open, visiting hospitals and old
people's homes, after-dinner speaking and judging fancy-
dress competitions. When I first started on television, I was
given some very good advice – never ever judge a baby
contest. I pass this on freely to any budding celebrity. To
this advice I would also add – never ever judge beauty
contests. In these two contests you can do no right, whoever
wins; everyone apart from the winner's relatives will
disagree with your decision and never more so than in a
baby contest.

Every mother rightly believes that her offspring is the
finest specimen ever to grace a nappy, but when I was asked
to judge the Ugliest Cat competition, I did not foresee many

problems. Let's face it, it is not a title that I would have thought many cat owners would be proud of. I had not taken into account the fact that prize money would be involved and also an appearance on television. Some people will do absolutely anything to appear on TV. I remember once when Chris Tarrant was sent out to conduct a campaign to stop people smoking, he went on to the streets of London with a camera crew and a bucket of water. When he spied somebody smoking, he approached them and said it was National Stub-It-Out-Week and if they would not comply, they must pay the forfeit. I would have thought that he was dicing with death, but apart from the fact that he is over six feet tall, I had forgotten the power of television. If the unfortunate smoker refused, Chris then poured the full contents of the bucket of icy cold water over their head. In no time at all, people were queueing up with lighted cigarettes, waiting to receive the same treatment. It was not a particularly warm day and I am convinced half the people did not smoke anyway, but thought that for those brief few seconds, they would reach stardom.

It was just the same with the owners of the ugly cats. There is an old saying that people grow to look like their dogs or unconsciously choose a dog which resembles themselves. I am not inferring that these particular cat owners were all Quasimodos but there was certainly a motley crew. It was hard to believe the history of some of the unfortunate cats. One-eyed three-legged cats were quite common in this competition. I always thought that contestants would at least try to be nice to a judge and some would even resort to bribery. The only thing that I got from this competition was a badly lacerated neck and back, and this was from the winner! This particular feline was about as graceful as a dustcart and had as much style as Worzel Gummidge. After he had been declared the winner and I was posing with him for photographs, he must have realised that he had finally reached star status and like all megastars before him it did not take him long to decide that he would no longer pose for photographs. In attempting to get away, he ran over my shoulder and lowered himself down my neck and back with all his front claws outstretched. Fortunately, none of the assembled press photographers got a picture of the actual incident, as I can imagine the captions which would have appeared in the newspapers the next day.

A few years ago, a strange photograph would not have been much use to a press photographer, particularly if the subject was not very clear, but now with the upsurge of the Sunday colour supplement magazines, a new market has been created for photographs of celebrities in unguarded positions. They use these with totally inappropriate captions to make the unfortunate subject look a complete fool. I once nearly fell into this particular sort of trap when I was offered a sum of £3,000 to pose for a few photographs. On the surface, this sounded a very good deal. I might add at this point that despite the seemingly large amount of money, these photographs were to be taken fully clothed, no Page Three for me! However, I found out just in time that the photographs were to be used in the more up-market glossy women's magazines to advertise sanitary towels. Can you imagine the copy? 'Sunny periods with Wincey.'

The cat pictures all appeared the next day with me smiling sweetly above the caption 'The Ugliest Cat'. I won't tell you who asked which was which, but his initials are N. O.

In the last two or three years, I have regularly flown home to the cottage at weekends, after suffering the inefficiency of British Rail and the ever increasing prices for far too long. Despite the fact that I live quite a way from Heathrow Airport, I discovered that it was just as economical in time and money for me to fly home. It was on one such occasion, on the Sunday flight returning from Teesside, that I needed to bring with me my adult male iguana. He was going on breeding loan to my friend Doctor Bernard Betts. He already had a thriving collection of green iguanas but was happy to take some fresh new blood. Early that weekend I had checked with the airline concerned that it would be possible for me to carry my iguana on the flight. I explained that I understood that I would not be allowed to keep it with me during the flight and that it would be carried in the pressurised and heated baggage compartment. My main concern was that I must be allowed to carry the box containing the iguana on and off the flight myself. Having worked in airports, I knew only too well the possible fate of any unac-companied piece of luggage. There is a story that goes 'Baggage handlers use luggage as a substitute for the toys they never had as children.' I was determined that no such disaster would happen to my iguana. They assured me that that would be fine and just to advise the stewardess on checking in that I had the iguana with me.

The embarcation at Teesside went without any problem and as I got on to the aircraft, the stewardess took my precious box, reassuring me about its safety. Arrival at Heathrow was a different matter. Normally, I choose a seat at the front of the aircraft and I am the first passenger to get off. I don't dislike flying but I resent the time wasted doing it and I am always eager for my journey to end. On this occasion, I waited for all the other passengers to disembark before collecting my box.

Alone in the front seat, I asked the stewardess to hand me my parcel at which point she hesitated and then explained that it was against airport regulations for me to carry my parcel from the aircraft. It must be taken by the baggage handlers to a separate entrance and I could reclaim it as normal in the baggage hall. I said that I already had been given firm reassurance that as I had carried the box on board at Teesside I would be allowed to carry it off at Heathrow. I explained it was not an animal needing quaran-tine and as I was on a domestic flight there should be no difficulty, but rules are rules. Despite all the promises I had received in the north, they counted for nothing against the blind officialdom of one of the world's busiest international airports.

Again I embarked on a one-woman campaign by refusing to leave the aircraft without my parcel. The young stew-ardess went off in search of the Number 1 and we re-enacted the whole conversation. She in turn sought out the first officer and Act 3 began. *He* sought out the captain and I was beginning to wish I had tape recorded the whole thing to save my patience and my breath. As the economics of flying demand, an aircraft must be quickly ready to take off again. The aircraft cleaners were by now coming on board and I was becoming a distinct embarrassment. Someone on board the aircraft must have radioed for assistance and Airport Security Ground Staff came to sort things out. Act 5. By now, I was becoming very impatient. If I had been foolish enough to attempt this without prior permission I would have understood all the fuss. I was wishing that at least I had had the foresight to get some kind of assurance in writing. Bits of paper with well-scrawled signatures on tend to impress uniformed officials.

Eventually the great British compromise was reached. The box containing my iguana would be carried off the aircraft by an official Heathrow baggage handler, but I would be allowed to walk alongside him and carry the other handle. Can you believe it? We must have looked completely ridiculous. Halfway across the tarmac, officialdom still had not ceased as the baggage handler attempted to abandon me and disappear with my iguana through a door marked 'Private, Staff Only'. I objected furiously and he explained that I had been allowed to accompany the iguana off the flight and must now go to the public waiting area to be reunited with my pet. I was not going to give in now and as he disappeared through the private door I hung on like grim death to the box and followed him. All the way through the 'No go' area, he protested that I was not allowed to be there but our procession continued all the same. It eventually terminated in the baggage reclaim hall at which point the handler released the other handle and I went on my way. Officialdom gone mad.

December

Oh Ding Dong Merrily on High, I wish this month was over! Humbug, Humbug! Let's face it, I am just not festive. It does tend to annoy me that at this time of year people go over board with charitable works and goodwill to all men and forget about it for the other eleven months, and what about the animals? Ever since I became well known, I have spent the whole of December trying to drum home the phrase used by the National Canine Defence League that 'A dog is for life, not just for Christmas'.

Of course, this does not apply only to dogs but to all animals and I try very hard to do my bit to discourage people from buying any kind of living creature as a Christmas present. Thousands of unwanted animals end up roaming the streets shortly after the Christmas festivities and animal sanctuaries up and down the country are inundated with new arrivals. The pet trade often does not help: every year products come on to the market which are not only unnecessary to an animal's well being but quite often in my opinion downright cruel. Who in heavens name could justify buying a mink coat for a dog? Where is the sense in anyone, however wealthy, spending hundreds of pounds on a diamond-encrusted gold collar? Who can convince me that any dog needs wellington boots?

One of the worst offenders of all has got to be the hamster playball. It is positively medieval and is a modern day equivalent of the torture chamber. This clear plastic ball comes in two parts, the idea being that you put your hamster inside, close it up and then he walks this never-ending treadmill around the floor. Very hygienic, no pee on the carpet and a hundred per cent washable but what about the hamster? He can't stop when he has had enough. He does not know how to open the ball. How many hamsters have been confined in such a horrific manner by ill-educated children and then discarded like all the other Christmas toys as something new attracts their attention? They should be totally banned.

How many so-called caring owners stuff their animals with unsuitable food as a Christmas treat? Vets all over the country will tell of the increased volume of choking animals, particularly dogs, being brought to their surgeries for emergency treatment after being given their own Christmas treat of turkey. All poultry bones are totally unsuitable, as they splinter and lodge in the unwary animal's throat.

Can you imagine what it must be like to be a tiny puppy bought as a Christmas gift for children who treat it as another toy? In one fell swoop it has been wrenched away from the security of the litter and the care of its mother to find itself in a new home, already in chaos due to Christmas festivities, noisier and more overcrowded than usual, often newly decorated and with a new carpet in readiness for the Christmas visitors and when in all the mayhem it is forgotten it is doubly punished for daring to pee on the new Axminster. Obviously there are some people who after careful consideration have decided that their family would like the addition of a new puppy. I always try to persuade them to buy all the puppy accessories on Christmas morning and wait until the calmer time after Christmas to bring home the new arrival. One of the best tips I was ever given to settle in a new puppy is to try and duplicate its mother: all you need is a hot water bottle and a ticking clock. Wrap these in a fluffy towel, put them in the puppy's basket and it should not take long before he snuggles up to the warmth and the 'heartbeat' of his substitute mum.

Winter is here with a vengeance by now and wildlife can suffer dreadfully. Ponds are frozen and herons and kingfishers find it increasingly difficult to survive. The tiniest birds are always the first to succumb and in severe winters blue tits and wrens suffer massive losses. Since I have been fortunate enough to be on television regularly, I have always used the opportunity to remind people to feed the birds. A few years ago I struck on an idea that I felt would not only increase my income but would also give me yet another opportunity to educate animal owners and ease the lot of some of the less well kept pets. I decided to take in boarders. I placed several ads in pet shops, offering holiday accommodation to all varieties of caged pets.

This was how I got to know Maurice. He was a large African grey parrot and his owners first brought him to me to stay for the Christmas holidays. It was at the time when we owned our first house and, according to the estate agents, to the rear there was a conservatory. In reality, it was more

159

like a half-glass shed tucked on to the back of the house.
But for my purposes it was ideal. It was small enough to
keep warm, and light and airy enough to accommodate a
few animals. Maurice moved in. On the first day he was
very quiet, but by the second morning he was showing
interest in most things around him. It was during that
morning while I was alone, replenishing his seed pot, that
Maurice first spoke to me. I was chattering away to him and
suddenly, very clearly, he said, 'Bonjour.' I was not quite
sure whether I had made a mistake as I knew that the family
who had delivered him were all true blue Englishmen and
there had been no mention of his linguistic abilities. Later
that day, I told Malcolm that Maurice had spoken to me in
French. He went out to the cage and stood for a good ten
minutes having a very one-sided broken French conversation. Maurice kept his beak firmly closed. The following
day, as I was feeding him again, I was given the continental
greeting. By the fourth consecutive morning, I thought I was
going mad as Maurice stubbornly insisted on saying nothing
at all when Malcolm was around. By the time the Christmas
holidays were over and his family came to collect him I was
getting quite disturbed. As soon as their car arrived, I ran
out to meet them and did not even bother to say hello but
asked if Maurice spoke French. They all laughed. Apparently, Maurice was quite fluent in fact, at one time the family
had lived in French West Africa, bought Maurice and
brought him back to England with them.

It was a few months later that I met Maurice again, when
he returned for his summer holidays. Again, on the first
day, he was very quiet and the second morning when I was
alone filling up his seed pot, thinking I was very clever,
conversing in French to this bilingual parrot, he surprised
me yet again. Not a bonjour was to be heard but this time
he said, 'Guten Morgen.' You could have knocked me over
with one of his bright red tail feathers. Needless to say,
Malcolm was not convinced. Maurice still firmly kept his
vows of silence while anyone else was around but as soon
as I was alone regaled me with much more of his German
vocabulary. This time when the family came back from
holidays, I was again very relieved to be reassured that I

was not going crazy: Maurice's new found trilingual abilities had been learnt from their eldest daughter who was practising for her German oral 'O' Level examination. It is strange how some birds constantly learn new things and others acquire a few words in the first years of life and never pick up anything new after that.

Molly, the citron-crested cockatoo, despite being extremely tame, has never achieved much in the way of vocabulary. The full extent of her speaking ability is Hello, Molly, Daddy and Da Di Da Di Da, and yet still she charms everyone who meets her. That is everyone except the other animals, over whom, despite her diminutive size, she rules with a ferocity that makes even the largest dog quake. When she has the free run of the living room, she immediately marks out invisible barriers which none of the other animals would dare to cross. Molly, like the macaw, prefers to walk around rather than use her powers of flight. She can regularly be seen running along biting the paws of the dogs, without any fear for her own safety, if they dare to cross one of her boundary lines. Rags makes a ridiculous sight trying to get through the living room by squeezing between the sofa and the wall so as to avoid another painful confrontation. Even he, with all his vicious tendencies, is terrified of the wrath of Molly.

One of the most endearing things about this bird is that even though she has the full power of flight and is regularly allowed to fly around the garden she always returns on command. I love to see her high up in the branches of the ancient oak tree at the bottom of the garden. At this time of year when the branches are bare, she can clearly be seen stripping away the bark searching for heaven knows what, scaring away the normal residents such as rooks and ring-necked doves. People out for a crisp winter's day walk have often been seen to stop and not believe their ears as this tiny voice can be heard somewhere in the distance shouting Daddy or singing her deranged little song. Whenever I have taken Molly to a television studio, she has behaved impeccably in rehearsal time but as soon as we start to record the programme she has never said a word. Once she disgraced herself very badly by biting the head of one of the tiny personal microphones that you can usually spot being worn by television presenters. Apart from the cost of the micro-phone, she was probably responsible for giving the sound engineer a dreadful headache.

Muriel Young, my great friend and mentor, once told me a story about working with a bird in a television studio. It was during her regular early evening slot aimed at children which included the much-loved puppets Fred Barker the dog and Ollie Beak the owl.

On one occasion – it was around this time of year when festivities were common – an actor was brought into the studio as part of the evening's entertainment to discuss a current play in which he was starring. The title of the play had something to do with being late. The actor was not awfully keen on the idea of appearing on television, as being a traditionalist theatre man he felt that anything other than treading the boards was not quite on. So Muriel had not had a particularly good time interviewing him. To lead on from one item to the next, the idea was that Ollie Beak should arrive late. Muriel sat there in front of the camera, immacu-late in her glamorous evening dress, bemoaning the fact that this dreadful little owl was incapable of being on time. For the third time she called out 'Ollie Beak, where are you, you dreadful little creature?' and at this point the owl was to arrive, operated by Wally Whyton hidden under the table at Muriel's feet. He duly appeared with his little cap at a jaunty angle on one side of his head and attached to one wing he had a helium-filled balloon bouncing around in the air. Muriel, in her terribly proper voice, scolded the naughty bird for arriving late and asked him where he had been.

'Sorry I'm late, Mu,' he said, 'but I have been to the Owl Ball,' to which she replied, 'Don't be silly, Ollie, owls don't have balls.' At this remark, the whole studio fell apart, the camera rocked as its operator creased up laughing, even the serious actor now sitting out of shot nearly choked. The rest of the crew collapsed in all directions and Wally had to stuff his other puppet Fred Barker in his mouth to stop himself laughing out loud. Fortunately, as is often the case, the perpetrator of the remark with the double meaning had not the faintest idea what she had said and so, completely alone, she continued to fill the next five minutes of air time which were left by reciting her well-remembered future pages from the *TV Times*. Five minutes can seem like a lifetime when you are struggling to fill it in a serious fashion as everyone around you collapses in hysterics. Eventually, the studio went off air and Muriel, by now furious, demanded to know what on earth was the matter with everyone. Eventually, the tearful cameraman managed to repeat her immortal line, 'Owls don't have balls.'

It is funny how things turn full circle and today, well over twenty years later, there seems again to be an upsurge of live television. With live television comes the inevitable series of faux pas. I am one of the fortunate people who are involved in live daily network broadcasts and in that situation mistakes are often made but that's another story.

I've tried to outline the last few years of my life with my animals in this my first book. I've deliberately left out the sad stories. This world is too full of misery most of the time. There have been many days when I've cried with sorrow and frustration because of my lack of skill or knowledge. As we grow older, we do grow wiser, and I'm learning all the time.

One of my more pleasant tasks in recent times was to become a Vice President of the Wildlife Hospitals Trust. Sue and Les Stocker, who run this wonderful establishment, have worked selflessly for many years to heal the sick and injured animals which are brought to them each year. Since working at TV-AM I have had to spend a great deal of time away from my own creatures, and I miss them a great deal. Working with Sue and Les eases the pain. They have just launched an ambitious scheme to create a teaching hospital for those people who want to learn more about the care of wildlife. They are in desperate need of funds and I hope to do my bit in helping them reach their goal.

We can all play our part, however small, in the care of the world and its creatures. The world is becoming more aware of its precious wild heritage. As an eternal optimist, I look forward to a bright future. Join me in helping to make it so.

USEFUL ADDRESSES

Jersey Wildlife Preservation Trust
Les Augres Manor
Trinity, Jersey, Channel Islands

British Chelonia Group
c/o 105 Burnham Lane
Slough, Berks,
SL1 6LA

Wildlife Hospitals Trust
1 Pemberton Close
Aylesbury, Bucks.
Telephone: Aylesbury 29860

National Canine Defence League
1 Pratt Mews
London NW1 0AD